(Christian Research Institute)

Guilty

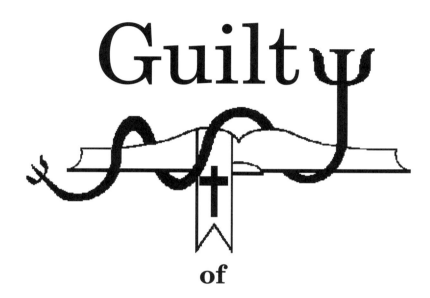

of

PSYCHOHERESY
?

Martin & Deidre Bobgan

EastGate Publishers

Scripture quotations are taken from the Authorized
King James Version of the Holy Bible.

CRI GUILTY OF PSYCHOHERESY?

Copyright © 1998 Martin and Deidre Bobgan
Published by EastGate Publishers
Santa Barbara, California

Library of Congress Catalog Card Number 98-92420
ISBN 0-941717-13-5

All rights reserved. No portion of this book may be reproduced
in any form without the written permission of the Publisher.

Printed in the United States of America

All scripture is given by inspiration of God, and is profitable for doctrine, for reproof, for correction, for instruction in righteousness:

That the man of God may be perfect, thoroughly furnished unto all good works.
(2 Timothy 3:16,17)

As ye have therefore received Christ Jesus the Lord, so walk ye in him:

Rooted and built up in him, and stablished in the faith, as ye have been taught, abounding therein with thanksgiving.

Beware lest any man spoil you through philosophy and vain deceit, after the tradition of men, after the rudiments of the world, and not after Christ.

For in him dwelleth all the fulness of the Godhead bodily.

(Colossians 2:6-9)

For a sample copy of a free newsletter about the intrusion of psychological counseling theories and therapies into Christianity, please write to:

PsychoHeresy Awareness Ministries
4137 Primavera Road
Santa Barbara, CA 93110

phone: 1-800-216-4696

e-mail: bobgan@psychoheresy-aware.org

Web Site Address:
www.psychoheresy-aware.org

CONTENTS

Introduction: 7
CRI's "Psychology & the Church" Series

1. Responding to Part One 21
   "Laying a Foundation for Discernment"

2. Responding to Part Two 45
   "The 'Biblical Counseling' Alternative"

3. Responding to Part Three 73
   "Can Psychology Be Integrated with
   Christianity?"

4. Responding to Part Four 109
   "The High Cost of Biblical Compassion
   and Commitment"

References..145

Introduction

CRI's "Psychology & the Church" Series

This current response to the Christian Research Institute (CRI) position on psychotherapy and its underlying psychologies seems like deja vu to us. Some years back Walter Martin, the founder of CRI, left the door open for hypnosis under certain conditions. Now the president of CRI, Hendrik (Hank) Hanegraaff, supports the position of Bob and Gretchen Passantino, which leaves the door open to psychotherapy and its underlying psychologies under certain conditions. The publication of the Passantinos' four articles establishes clearly that this is the CRI position. And, just as Walter Martin was in error about hypnosis, so too Hank Hanegraaff is in error about psychotherapy.

Hanegraaff and the Passantinos may protest that there is no relation between hypnosis and psychotherapy and therefore no relation between Walter Martin's leaving the door open to hypnosis and Hanegraaff's leaving the door open to psychotherapy. However, there is a definite connection. In a section titled "Mesmerism: The Beginning of American Psychology," the American Psychological Association's book on the *History of Psychotherapy: A Century of Change* says:

> Historians have found several aspects of mesmerism and its offshoots that set the stage for 20th-century psychotherapy. It promoted ideas that are quintessentially American and have become permanent theoretical features of our 20th-century psychological landscape (Freedheim, 32).

In his book *Mesmerism and the American Cure of Souls*, Robert Fuller describes how the thrust of mesmerism changed directions as it came to America (Fuller, 46,47). Its promoters garnered great expectations of psychological and spiritual advantage. Non-Christians especially welcomed its promises for self-improvement, spiritual experience, and personal fulfillment. Fuller says that mesmerism offered Americans "an entirely new and eminently attractive arena for self-discovery—their own psychological depths" and that "its theories and methods promised to restore individuals, even unchurched ones, into harmony with the cosmic scheme" (Fuller, 104). The anticipated possibility of discovering and developing human potential, which emerged from mesmerism, stimulated the growth and expansion of psychotherapy, positive thinking, the human potential movement, hypnosis, and mind-science religions. Fuller's description of mesmerism in America accurately portrays twentieth-century psychotherapy.

Mesmer's far reaching influence gave an early impetus to scientific-sounding religious alternatives to Christianity. Moreover, his work established the trend of medicalizing the mind and replacing religion with treatment and therapy. Mesmer gave the world another false religion and another false hope. Psychiatrist Thomas Szasz describes Mesmer's influence:

> Insofar as psychotherapy as a modern "medical technique" can be said to have a discoverer, Mesmer was that person. Mesmer stands in the same sort of relation to Freud and Jung as Columbus stands in relation to Thomas Jefferson and John Adams. Columbus stumbled onto a continent that the founding fathers subsequently transformed into the political entity known as the United States of America. Mesmer stumbled onto the literalized use of the leading scientific metaphor of his age for explaining and exorcising all manner of human problems and passions, a rhetorical device that the founders of modern depth psychology subsequently transformed into the pseudomedical entity known as psychotherapy (Szasz, 43).

Because of their position on psychotherapy and its underlying psychologies, CRI and the Passantinos are guilty of what we call *psychoheresy*. We coined the term *psychoheresy* with the following definition: a psychological heresy, a heresy because it is a departure from the Word of God and from the fundamental truth of the Gospel, a psychological heresy because the departure is the use of and support of unproven and unscientific psychological opinions of men instead of absolute confidence in the biblical truth of God. CRI, through the Passantinos, leaves the door open to the integration of secular psychological counseling theories and therapies with the

Bible. These teachings have become so accepted in Christian schools, seminaries, churches, missionary organizations, books, radio and other media that many Christians assume such psychological ideas are true and even biblical. Thus, the tentacles of the psychological way have strangled the thinking of many Christians. CRI must now accept part of the responsibility for the church's ongoing capitulation to and use of psychotherapy.

Bob and Gretchen Passantinos' four-part series on "Psychology & the Church" was published in the *Christian Research Journal*. The four-article series represents nothing new or revelational about either psychology or about what the Passantinos refer to as the "Biblical Counseling Movement (BCM)." Their position supports the psychotherapists' view rather than that of the psychotherapy critics. There is little that a professional psychotherapist would disagree with in the Passantino articles and the Christian psychologists are no doubt delighted that the Christian Research Institute (CRI) has left the door open to continued business as usual for professional psychotherapy.

While the Passantinos will protest, stating that their articles are critical of psychology, all of the integrationists named in their articles have also been critical in some way of psychology. So to say the Passantinos are critical of psychology separates them from none of the integrationists on that count.

In their series the Passantinos provide enough information to condemn the idea that psychotherapy is science, but seem to be confused about it. They reveal enough about psychotherapy to condemn it as being of any value for Christians, but avoid doing so. They criticize certain theories and practices of psychotherapy, but do not link their charges with the specific individuals and organizations involved. They laud certain theories and practices of psychotherapy, but, with only a one brief paragraph exception, they refrain from saying which individuals and organizations they recommend. While they expose many of the problems of psychotherapy, they fail to warn about the widespread encroachment of psychotherapeutic theories and practices throughout the church. Their oleaginous approach undermines the effect of the evidence they do present. The Passantinos give evidence of knowing enough to shut down the psych-industry in all its forms throughout the church, but instead they tenaciously hang onto the idea that it's fine if done their way.

A repeated recommendation in the Passantino series is the open door to psychotherapy and its underlying psychologies under certain conditions. Even with these conditions, they are not able to produce one integrationist who would admit to violating the Bible with his theories and techniques. Worse yet, in one brief paragraph they name two individuals (William Backus and James Dobson) as models of what they recommend, but these two individuals are found to be grossly unbiblical. The Passantinos' failed formula with those two individuals leaves them with zero individuals who exemplify what they recommend. With zero integrationists whom the Passantinos can name that admit they violate the Bible with their therapies and techniques and zero individuals who actually comply with their recommendations when tested, the Passantinos have come up with zero reasons for leaving the psychotherapeutic door open. Their recommendations add up to one big zero for God's people.

The Passantinos have enough information to close the door on psychotherapy for Christians, but they do not. The question for the reader throughout is: Have the Passantinos provided adequate scientific and biblical evidence to support their leaving the door open for psychotherapy under the conditions they describe? We demonstrate that they have failed to do so. As we say later, "The Passantinos promise much . . . but provide little. With all their razzle-dazzle about using psychology under certain conditions, they were not able to give one example of an insight from psychotherapy and its underlying psychologies that is of any use to the Christian, and they could not name one individual whose work would demonstrate what they claim. These facts alone should condemn the entire series."

Even before the Passantino articles appeared, many of us accurately predicted their substance. Their leaving the door open to psychotherapy and its underlying psychologies and their use of John Coe's psychotheology* to support their own position were no surprise. And, who is Coe, whose theology dominates the CRI/Passantino position? Coe is a professor at the Rosemead School of Psychology, which produces numerous integrationists who are active participants in psychoheresy. What else would one expect from a faculty member at a school that dispenses and promotes psychoheresy? In our critique of Part Two, we present a diametrically different view than the CRI/Passantino/Coe psychotheology.

After the first Passantino article appeared we wrote the following letter to the editor of the *Christian Research Journal*:

> In the first of a four-part series on psychology and the church, the Passantinos identify us. We are unabashedly opposed to psychotherapy and its underlying psychologies for both biblical and research reasons, described in a number of our books. Unless they have changed their minds, the Passantinos are pro-psychotherapy and its underly-

---

* A theology that leaves the door open to psychotherapy and its underlying psychologies.

ing psychologies. In other words, they support the integration position. The Passantinos' articles need to be read with their pro-psychology bias in mind.

The editor suggested that we hold off responding until the series was completed. The editor mentioned that psychotherapy would be critiqued in the third installment. We did not need to wait until that third installment as we had already accurately identified the Passantinos' position.

After the Passantino series first came out we were called by someone in Texas whom we had never met and did not know, but who has an apologetic ministry. He asked if we were willing to have a debate with the Passantinos on his radio program. We immediately agreed and waited for confirmation of the date. After much time had elapsed we were told that the Passantinos declined, even though they were repeatedly contacted and given an option on the date.

While the Passantinos, the integrationists, and most people in the church support the open door to psychotherapy, many secularists are closing the door on it. Dr. Tana Dineen is a clinical psychologist who has written a book titled *Manufacturing Victims: What the Psychology Industry is doing to People*. Dineen relates in detail how the psychological manufacturing of victims takes place. She differentiates between real victims and the ones manufactured by the "Psychology Industry," which involves a blurring between the two and spreads a net to include virtually everyone. She concludes her book by saying:

> The Psychology Industry can neither reform itself from within nor should it be allowed to try. It should be stopped from doing what it is doing to people, from manufacturing victims. And while the Psychology Industry is being dismantled, people can boycott

psychological treatment, protest the influence of the Psychology Industry and resist being manufactured into victims (Dineen, 309).

Dineen's conclusion also applies to the "Christian Psychology" industry. The following was admitted at a meeting of the Christian Association for Psychological Studies (CAPS), which is an organization of psychologists who are professing Christians:

> We are often asked if we are "Christian psychologists" and find it difficult to answer since we don't know what the question implies. We are Christians who are psychologists but at the present time there is no acceptable Christian psychology that is markedly different from non-Christian psychology. It is difficult to imply that we function in a manner that is fundamentally distinct from our non-Christian colleagues . . . as yet there is not an acceptable theory, mode of research or treatment methodology that is distinctly Christian (Sutherland & Poelstra).

As more and more Christians are supporting psychotherapy and its underlying psychologies over the past 25 years, more and more secularists are coming against it, because they are willing to pay serious attention to the research. It is a tragedy when conclusions reached by many secular researchers would lead one to close the door on professional psychotherapy and its underlying psychologies, while the Passantinos and integrationists reach conclusions that leave the door open to such practices. Any objective reading of the Passantinos' series will reveal that this complex issue is simplistically concluded to the advantage of the psychotherapist and at the expense of the church.

Because the Passantinos' warnings finger no one and their qualifications for seeing a therapist are so easily confirmed by integrationists, no one will stop from using even the most corrupt of therapies or therapists. If Hanegraaff wrote his critiques in a similar fashion, the door would be left open to all kinds of aberrations, heresies and cults, under certain conditions of course.

Prior to the appearance of the Passantinos' articles, we made a presentation to Hanegraaff and his staff on the subject of psychoheresy. CRI sent the following reply to those who inquired about their position on psychology and the church:

> CRI is still in the process of evaluating the proper relationship between psychology and the Christian church and formally establishing a position on this controversial topic. We have met with prominent people on both sides of this debate and it remains an issue that must be carefully studied and assessed. If you would like information on this subject from opposing points of view so you can prayerfully study and come to your own conclusions, we recommend materials from Martin and Deidre Bobgan (anti-psychology) and John Coe (pro-psychology).

CRI was correct in saying that our position is "anti-psychology" and Coe's position is "pro-psychology." The prominence of Coe's pro-psychology theology in the Passantinos' series confirms that CRI chose the pro-psychology position. In opposition to Coe's pro-psychology paper, Hanegraaff had a copy of a paper opposing Coe's position, which was written by Doug Bookman, a professor at The Master's College.

In a letter to Hanegraaff one of us said:

I would like to suggest that you sponsor a debate at Rosemead Graduate School on this issue. I have tried in the past to arrange such a debate or even to speak there with no success. If your staff has heard them and us separately, why not now put the two sides out in public together? . . . I believe you would do the church a great service if you would sponsor such a debate. Please give it some thought and prayer. I look forward to your reply.

Hanegraaff never replied. It cannot be said that Hanegraaff lacked information to make a decision regarding what should be the CRI position on psychotherapy and its underlying psychologies. But, it can be said that his decision is harmonious with the many integrationists we have accused of psychoheresy over the years and would certainly be applauded by the many integrationists quoted in the Passantinos' articles.

Leaving the door open to psychotherapy and its underlying psychologies is an overwhelmingly popular position in the church. Many are satisfied and others are ecstatic about the CRI/Passantino position on the integration of psychology and the Bible. It is always difficult to combat the popular socio-cultural mores of a society, but it is more difficult to fight against the absorption of these mores into the church. Admittedly, we are presenting a minority view and unfortunately we are left with proving the case against something for which the case has never been made to begin with.

Based on hundreds of research studies, Dr. Robyn Dawes, professor at Carnegie-Mellon University and a widely recognized researcher on psychological evaluations, declares:

> . . . there is no positive evidence supporting the efficacy of professional psychology. There are anecdotes,

there is plausibility, there are common beliefs, yes—but there is no good evidence (Dawes, 58).

While the Passantinos refer to Dawes' book in a footnote, they give little evidence to suggest they read it.

Those who have been paying attention to the research have been sounding alarms about psychotherapy. In his book *The Myth of Psychotherapy*, Dr. Thomas Szasz warns:

> My point is rather that many, perhaps most, so-called psychotherapeutic procedures are harmful for the so-called patients . . . and that all such interventions and proposals should therefore be regarded as evil until they are proven otherwise (Szasz, xxiii).

Michael Scriven, when he was a member of the American Psychological Association Board of Social and Ethical Responsibility, questioned "the moral justification for dispensing psychotherapy, given the state of outcome studies which would lead the FDA to ban its sale if it were a drug" (Scriven, 96). The outcome studies continue to confirm the results upon which the remarks by Szasz and Scriven were based.

After reviewing all the research, one could conclude that professional psychotherapy is one of the biggest and most vicious ripoffs that has ever been perpetrated on the American public and that it is one of the greatest deceptions in the church today. When he was president of the Association for Humanistic Psychology, Dr. Lawrence LeShan said, "Psychotherapy may be known in the future as the greatest hoax of the twentieth century." It may also be known as the greatest heresy of twentieth-century Christianity.

Even *The Family Therapy Networker*, a publication by and for psychological counselors, is honest enough to report:

> Money is not the only worm in the golden apple of old-time therapeutic practice. Books citing the irrelevance, incompetence, venality and even downright criminality of therapists have become this year's literary growth industry, aimed at a mass market of apparently disillusioned therapy consumers. At the same time, a plethora of outcome research studies paints a troubling picture of the profession, finding virtually no empirical evidence that any one therapy model is significantly more or less effective than any other.
>
> Finally, as if this weren't enough bad news, therapists over the past 10 or 15 years have been made to realize just how culture bound, parochial and downright discriminatory some of their most cherished theories and models actually have been (Nov/Dec 1994, p. 10).

Because the efficacy of professional psychotherapy has not been fully demonstrated, Alexander Astin contends that "psychotherapy should have died out. But it did not. It did not even waver. Psychotherapy had, it appeared, achieved *functional autonomy*" (Astin, 62, italics his). Functional autonomy occurs when a practice continues after the circumstances which supported it are gone. Astin is suggesting that psychotherapy has become self perpetuating because there is no support for its efficacy. Astin concludes his comments with the following dismal note:

> If nothing else, we can be sure that the principle of functional autonomy will permit psychotherapy to

survive long after it has outlived its usefulness as a personality laboratory (Astin, 65).

Professional psychotherapy has not been affirmed by scientific scrutiny and only remains because of the usual inertia that results when a movement becomes established and then entrenched. Worse yet, because integrationists have mixed psychotherapeutic theories with the very Word of God, many professing Christians have incorporated these notions into their belief system and added them to the scenery of their so-called Christian world view.

In *The Emperor's New Clothes* after the little boy cried out, "He has no clothes!" the people knew that what the boy said was true. The greatest tragedy was not the discovery (no clothes), but the continuation of the deception by the emperor. The story goes on:

> The Emperor squirmed. All at once he knew that what the people said was right. "All the same," he said to himself, "I must go on as long as the procession lasts." So the Emperor kept on walking, his head held higher than ever. And the faithful minister kept on carrying the train that wasn't there (Andersen).

And so, like the naked emperor, psychotherapy and all its psychologies will go on "as long as the procession lasts." And, CRI and the Passantinos will probably continue in that charade of a parade "as long as the procession lasts." For many of us the procession is over. The cure of minds (psychotherapy) never was and never will be a satisfactory replacement for the cure of souls (biblical ministry).

Perhaps the Passantinos consider that their openness to psychotherapy and its underlying psychologies demonstrates open-mindedness. However, Jonathan Adler, a professor of philosophy at Brooklyn College and the Graduate Center of the City University of New York, has said, "What truly marks an open-minded person is the willingness to follow where evidence leads. The open-minded person is willing to defer to impartial investigations rather than to his or her own predilections" (Adler, 44). The Passantinos' lack of open-mindedness should leave many open-mouthed at their open-door recommendations and conclusions.

Some of those who have researched the effectiveness of psychotherapy have likened themselves to the doggedly optimistic boy in the old joke, who was found cheerfully digging his way through a large pile of horse manure. When asked why, he responded, "With all of this horse manure, there must be a pony in here somewhere!" The Passantinos' hoped-for pony is not there; what you see in this illustration is what you get.

Much more could be written about the failure of the Passantinos to deal objectively and extensively with the complexity of the issues involved. This book only touches upon some of their errors. To make it convenient for the reader to compare our response to the Passantinos' articles, we respond to each article (Part One, Part Two, etc.) in the series and use the same section headings as they do, though for the sake of brevity we do not respond to all of them.

While the Passantinos have written on a variety of issues, the psychology and the church issue is one they should have left alone. Their many failings in this four-part series are probably traceable to their "predilections" about psychology and were possibly supported and influenced by their friendships with certain individuals. Their foregone conclusions were visible throughout all of the four parts and were no doubt the driving force behind their use of so many logical fallacies to "prove" their position.

1

Responding to Part One

"Laying a Foundation for Discernment"

The first article, designated Part One in the CRI/Passantino series on psychology and the church, is titled "Laying a Foundation for Discernment"

"The Complexity of the Problem"

The Passantinos mention two extreme positions with respect to psychology: "total acceptance or total rejection" (22). They represent themselves with the following statement: "[Psychology] is a complex subject and the lines must be drawn carefully to produce a responsible and balanced evaluation of it" (22).

A major problem with the Passantino series is that they admit psychology is a complex subject, but they demonstrate ignorance about many of its complexities and fail to deal with some of them, except in a very superficial manner. They suggest that they are drawing lines carefully, but we shall demonstrate that they have drawn lines carelessly and even recklessly at times. They believe they have produced a responsible and balanced evaluation of psychology, but they have merely used the series to promote their own views.

The Passantinos use the word *complex* as a means of demonstrating that "total acceptance or total rejection" is too simplistic. The fact that some of the most scholarly writers in the field have dealt thoroughly with the complexities and present an entirely different view than the Passantinos has apparently escaped them. We could quote literally hundreds of studies having to do with the questionability of the very practice for which the Passantinos have left an open door.

Not dealing with the extensive research having to do with the efficacy of psychotherapy and its underlying psychologies is a giant failing in the Passantino series. This failure demonstrates that they have not dealt with the needed facets of the subject's complexity, which would hamstring their ability to draw lines carefully. Their oversight, due to bias, unfamiliarity, or insufficient knowledge, is probably why they produced an unbalanced series.

In their section "The Complexity of the Problem," the Passantinos present three simplistic testimonials, none of which rejects psychology. Instead of presenting the complexity of the problem, their three examples introduce confusion. Each example contains simplistic and false information, which the Passantinos fail to clarify or refute anywhere in the series. More could be said about each of the examples to demonstrate the errors; however, we will give only one quote from each with a comment. Since each example is about a friend of the Passantinos, we will refer to them that way.

In the first anecdote Friend One gives reasons why Christians would rather go to Alcoholics Anonymous and asks a rhetorical question, "Why do we wonder when Christians who abuse alcohol go to secular programs when they are not welcome in their own churches?" (22). This is only a partial truth. There are numerous churches that welcome and work with sinners of all sorts, including substance abusers. In addition, there are numerous Christian organizations that provide ministry to such individuals. Apparently the Passantinos are ignorant of such programs and are not aware of the great spiritual danger posed by Alcoholics Anonymous and other similar programs.

The research is clear about AA; it provides no advantage over other such programs and it presents a world view alien to Christianity. For instance, *The Journal of Studies on Alcohol* (January 1997) reported that "one of the largest clinical experiments ever conducted," sponsored by the National Institute on Alcohol Abuse and Alcoholism, found, in comparing individuals in various programs (including those in hospital settings and those on the outside), that none of the treatments was more successful than the others. The only differences in success had to do with other factors, such as personal motivation and social environment. The Passantinos' description of Friend One also sounds contradictory. They describe him as one who is involved in AA and also as one who "pursued a strong biblical counseling practice." In other words this person is evidently one who purports to be a biblical counselor (using the Scriptures), but who seeks personal help from an unbiblical system.

The second anecdote is about a man whose son did not do well in psychotherapy. Friend Two asks, "If I dismiss all psychology because it didn't work with my son, does that mean I must dismiss the Bible because biblical counseling didn't work either?" (22). Throughout their four articles the Passantinos resort to a number of logical fallacies to promote their views. Friend Two's reasoning contains a logical fallacy called false analogy. One logic text explains:

> An argument from analogy draws a conclusion about something on the basis of an analogy with or resemblance to some other thing. The assumption is that if two or more things are alike in some respects, they are alike in some other respect (Johnson, 256).

In regard to a false analogy the text says:

> To recognize the fallacy of false analogy, look for an argument that draws a conclusion about one thing, event, or practice on the basis of its analogy or resemblance to others. The fallacy occurs when the analogy or resemblance is not sufficient to warrant the conclusion (Johnson, 258).

This type of psychology is comprised of the unproven opinions of men, whereas the Bible is the truth of God. Friend Two is equating "science falsely so-called" with the very truth from God and then coming to a conclusion about psychology. In addition, pragmatism is the unbiblical standard of evaluation here, rather than truth.

Friend Three, a mental health professional who "hesitates to identify himself as a Christian," wonders, "How can I believe the Bible has all the answers for fulfilled personal living when people who 'swear by it' are so messed up?" (22). Apparently this mental health professional is not aware of the "mental health" and other benefits attributed to believers and ignorant of the many problems that mental health professionals themselves have. We could provide the Passantinos with much research on this, but we will refer to only one article, "Why Shrinks Have So Many Problems" by Robert Epstein, Ph.D., in which he reports, "Suicide, stress, divorce—psychologists and other mental health professionals may actually be more screwed up than the rest of us." Near the beginning of his article Epstein says:

> Sure Freud was peculiar, and, yes, I'd heard that Jung had had a nervous breakdown. But I'd always assumed that—rumors to the contrary notwithstanding—mental health professionals were probably fairly healthy.
> Turns out I was wrong.

The following revealing quotes are from Epstein's article:

> A number of surveys . . . reveal some worrisome statistics about therapists' lives and well-being. At least three out of four therapists have experienced major distress within the past three years, the principal cause being relationship problems. More than 60 percent may have suffered a clinically significant depression at some point in their lives, and nearly half admitted that in the weeks following a personal crisis they're unable to deliver quality care. As for psychiatrists, a 1997 study by Michael Klag, M.D., found that the divorce rate for psychiatrists who graduated from Johns Hopkins University School of Medicine between 1948 and 1964 was 51 percent—higher than that of the general population of that era, and substantially higher than the rate in any other branch of medicine. . . .

> According to psychologist David Lester, Ph.D., director of the Center for the Study of Suicide, mental health professionals kill themselves at an abnormally high rate. . . .
> One out of every four psychologists has suicidal feelings at times, according to one survey, and as many as one in 16 may have attempted suicide (Epstein, 59).

We have often said that mature believers are capable of providing far better support for troubled people than psychotherapists. Moreover, Friend Three's goal of "fulfilled personal living" falls far short of the biblical goal of glorifying God and being conformed to the image of Christ.

In their footnotes the Passantinos say, "These friends' stories are meant as illustrations of the complexity of the issue. They are not presented here as proof or documentation for any position." However, these three anecdotes are not "illustrations of the complexities of the issues." They are examples of simplistic thinking on the part of the Passantinos and their three friends. Moreover, these stories demonstrate a bias on the Passantinos' part to present these simplicities as complexities. We can only feel sorry for the three friends whom the Passantinos made no effort, at least in print, to guide out of their confusion and simplistic thinking. In presenting these as illustrations, the Passantinos sound as confused as their friends and do a disservice to their readers by adding confusion rather than clarity to a complex issue.

Instead of giving the testimonies of these three friends, the Passantinos would have better served God's people by quoting some testimonies from the other side. One Christian woman, who had been through the psychological and psychiatric system for years and is now a critic of it, says the following:

The type of relationship established in therapy is one that needs close Biblical examination. Doing so reveals a closer resemblance to prostitution than to Biblical love. A relationship which ought to be founded on love is converted to one of business. Prostitution takes an intimate relationship which should never involve money and establishes a profit-making business. The counselee is more of an inanimate object than a Christian brother in need of our ministry, prayer, and loving service. Friendship is out of the question; there is no genuine involvement or commitment that extends beyond the professional obligation. The Bible instructs us to serve one another in love, to esteem others ahead of self, and to preach the gospel without charge (Dewart, 4).

This woman has become theologically trained and has written extensively on the subject of "Psychology & the Church." She would have been a far better choice to write this series for CRI. However, she would not have presented the same view as CRI found in the Passantinos.

After their three stories, the Passantinos say: "Indeed, psychology is one of the most controversial and divisive issues in the church today" (22). Actually for most people it is a non-issue, because most professing Christians are eager promoters and consumers of psychotherapeutic ideas and techniques through books, tapes, seminars, seminaries, and radio shows, as well as through professional counseling. They may feel irritated that a few people speak out against it, but it is far from being the "most controversial." One of the most serious? Yes! One of the most controversial? Definitely not! For those who profit from other people's problems, the controversy thus far has posed little threat to their income. As we have documented elsewhere, both the secular and Christian psychology industries are thriving (Bobgan, *The End of "Christian Psychology,"* Ch 1; *PAL*, V4N6).

"The Scope of Psychology"

The Passantinos understand, but at times confuse, the difference between psychotherapy with its underlying psychologies, on the one hand, and the general word *psychology,* which covers a multitude of fields and numerous other individuals, on the other hand. They define the difference between the terms *psychology* and *psychotherapy* and say that their focus "in these articles will be on (though not limited to) psychotherapy" (23).

They begin this section by properly defining the word *psychology* and then wrongly accusing individuals who condemn the religious nature of *psychotherapy.* They rightly speak of the "evolving nature of language" but then state:

> Those who use the term *psychology* today do not generally mean to make any religious statements about the human spirit or soul, but instead are referring to the nontangible personal aspects of human beings (22).

However, it is not just the etymology of the word *psychology,* but rather its current usage in the field of psychotherapy that is of concern to us. Colossians 2:8 warns: "Beware lest any man spoil you through philosophy and vain deceit, after the tradition of men, after the rudiments of the world, and not after Christ." This warning applies to psychotherapeutic psychology and its philosophical origins.

Dr. Thomas Szasz is probably one of the most distinguished psychiatrists in the world. In endorsing one of our earlier books, Szasz said:

Although I do not share the Bobgans' particular religious view, I do share their conviction that the human relations we now call "psychotherapy," are, in fact, matters of religion—and that we mislabel them as "therapeutic" at great risk to our spiritual well-being. This is an important book.

We could quote numerous others who see psychotherapy and its underlying psychologies as religion. Interestingly, most of them are atheists. Elsewhere Szasz has said:

Herein lies one of the supreme ironies of modern psychotherapy: it is not merely a religion that pretends to be a science, it is actually a fake religion that seeks to destroy true religion (Szasz, 27,28).

He warns about the "implacable resolve of psychotherapy to rob religion of as much as it can, and to destroy what it cannot" (Szasz, 188).

The Passantinos have misrepresented the position of those who call this type of psychology *religion* by first presenting an evolution of language argument, which has nothing to do with the substance of the criticism, and then by deflecting the substance of the criticism of psychotherapy by using an argument about the whole field of psychology. They may not know that the American Psychological Association has over 50 divisions. There is a mixture of science and pseudoscience among the various divisions and practitioners. The Passantinos' failure to present and confront this variety reveals an inadequate understanding of the complexities involved throughout the disciplines of psychology. They set out to present the complexities but through important omissions, they have confused rather than clarified.

"The Origin of Psychology"

In the previous section the Passantinos quote a "leading Christian textbook" definition of *psychology* as a "scientific study" (23). They begin this section by saying, "Psychology is among the youngest sciences" (23). In this section they mishmashedly present the laboratory work of William Wundt along with the description of five systems of thought in psychology. All of this follows their initial reference to psychology as science. They make no needed distinction in this brief history as to what is and what is not science. Their only criticism is directed at mental health counselors when they "pragmatically choose what they like or think will work from any of the three major branches of psychotherapy" (23). The Passantinos' criticism is directed at therapists using, with a single client, a variety of approaches that have "rational underpinnings" that are "mutually exclusive" (23). Because they sometimes raise the practice of psychotherapy to the level of science and limit their criticism to only certain practices, such as irresponsible eclecticism, they leave the door open to psychotherapy. One sees both criticisms and compliments in this section, which tends to leave their readers confused and vulnerable. Because of the manner in which psychotherapy is presented and practiced, a Christian, after having read the Passantinos' articles and thereby being assured that existing problems are resolvable, could easily step through the door into some of the worst kinds of psychotherapy.

"Psychology and the Scientific Method"

In this section the Passantinos discuss the scientific method. As important as it is to discuss the scientific method, it is more important to discuss whether psychotherapy itself is science. While it is true that research can employ the scientific method, it does not follow that whatever is being investigated is scientific. Many nonscientific and even questionable practices, such as E.S.P., biorhythms, fingertip reading, and psychic phenomena, have been investigated by scientific research procedures. The scientific method has been used to investigate everything from art to Zen and from prayer to politics. We certainly would not call all of these *science*.

The Passantinos say, "However, consistent, comprehensive application of the scientific method is impossible in psychology because of certain unique features" (23,24) They give several excellent reasons why. While what they have written in this section should lead them to condemn psychotherapy as science, they continue to leave the door open by quoting the summary by Paul Meier et al. of Mary Stewart VanLeeuwen's position on psychology as science. The Passantinos quote Meier et al. as saying, "VanLeeuwen doubts whether that approach used by physicists and biologists is appropriate for the study of human behavior and thinking" (36). So, instead of ending this section with a condemnation of psychotherapy as science, they end with a question as to whether or not the scientific paradigm is an appropriate one to evaluate the practice of psychotherapy. The typical response of therapists is either to ignore the research or point out the shortcomings of the research method. Disregarding and devaluating research serve to keep the therapists in business.

The serious weaknesses in their articles seem to be due to having an agenda that would allow some warnings to be sounded about some of the errors of psychology but would prevent closing the door to all psychotherapies and their underlying theories. That would explain the absence of an adequate representation of the extensive research about psychotherapy as science. For example many psychologists have made a case for the idea that psychotherapy is merely personal opinions offered as science. Dr. Linda Riebel has said, "theories of human nature reflect the theorist's personality as he or she externalizes it or projects it onto humanity at large" (Riebel, 90). Dr. Harvey Mindess says in his book titled *Makers of Psychology: The Personal Factor*, "It is my intention to show how the leaders of the field portray humanity in their own image and how each one's theories and techniques are a means of validating his own identity" (Mindess, 15).

Failure to truly present the complexity of the issue by including such research permits the Passantinos to conform what they do know to their own presuppositions about psychotherapy.

"Psychotherapy"

The Passantinos discuss psychotherapy in this section and make a very interesting statement:

> Some psychotherapies, especially some of the cognitive ones (and certainly we would hope ones practiced by Christians), intend to improve not simply one's feelings, but also one's abilities to act individually and socially in reality (36).

One can only guess at why the Passantinos elevate the cognitive therapies over the others. They may have heard this from one of their "mental health" worker friends. However, there is no research reason for doing so. It is unfortunate that the Passantinos often give personal opinion unsubstantiated by research. The Passantinos often state something that begs a footnote or a quote, but none is to be found. The Passantinos owe the reader a footnote here but do not provide one. Their statement, about cognitive psychotherapies being "especially" the ones to accomplish what they say, would certainly not be supported in the research.

According to the *Handbook of Psychotherapy and Behavior Change* (*Handbook*), what is referred to in the research literature as the "Dodo Bird Verdict" still holds. After an extensive review of the literature on outcomes of the various schools of therapies, several researchers "suggested a verdict similar to that of the DoDo bird in *Alice in Wonderland*: 'Everyone has won and all must have prizes'" (Bergin, 156). The *Handbook* states that "meta-analytic methods have now been extensively applied to large groups of comparative studies, and these reviews generally offer similar conclusions (i.e., little or no difference between therapies)" (Bergin, 156). In its conclusions, the *Handbook* lists "psychotherapy research achievements." One of the ten listed is the following: "Demonstrating the relative equivalence in outcome for a large number of therapies, therapeutic modalities, and temporal arrangements" (Bergin, 828). This is repeatedly referred to in the research literature as "The Equal Outcomes Phenomenon" (Bergin, 822).

The Passantinos return to two early themes by saying:

> The primary explanation for this wide variation and inconsistency in psychotherapeutic practice is that most counselors use what appears to work at various times with various patients, without strict regard to the foundational schools from which the techniques developed, and without the scientific objectivity and testing one would expect from a practitioner of a science (36)

While the variety of psychotherapies can be used to condemn the profession as a whole, the Passantinos use it to condemn individual therapists with whom they may disagree, and yet they leave the door open to those practitioners who are eclectic, as long as they do it scientifically—whatever that means. One can also see that the Passantinos themselves are guilty of not paying "strict regard to the foundational schools from which the techniques developed" when they made their positive statement about cognitive psychotherapy.

The Passantinos' reference to an expectation from a "practitioner of a science" repeats again their error of crediting psychotherapy with being science, a subject with which they have only superficially dealt and which they conveniently turned into a non-issue with the reference to VanLeeuwen's remark.

The *Handbook* says, "Therapists identify themselves as eclectics more frequently than any other orientation." The *Handbook* then says:

> At the same time, the use of the term eclectic does not have any precise operational meaning beyond the general definition of selecting from diverse sources what is considered best for the individual case. The fact that two psychotherapists identify themselves as eclectics does not in any way indicate that they would treat a specific case in exactly the same way (Bergin, 7).

The *Handbook* reveals a further serious problem with eclectic psychotherapy when it says, "Eclecticism does not represent any truly systematic view, and thus research on this approach has been minimal and in fact is not really possible" (Bergin, 7). If one is selling a product or a procedure, in this case psychotherapy, and there is a direct or implied benefit (such as help, relief, cure), then there should be some scientific validation for its use. None exists. If these psychotherapists were truly "practitioners of science," they would cease practicing these approaches because they are not scientifically validated.

The Passantinos refer both to the benefits and weaknesses of the diversity of approaches in psychotherapy. They first say:

> The benefit of such [psychotherapeutic] diversity is that counselors can acknowledge their clients' unique problems, emotional and mental states, and abilities to make changes in their own lives (36).

Later, in Part Three of their series, the Passantinos say that the psychotherapists "pick and choose from hundreds of different systems, techniques, methods, schools, and ideas, applying 'what works' in individual cases with different people with different problems" (Part 3, 22). These statements seem to contradict their earlier criticism of the underlying theories (23).

Evidently the Passantinos are not in touch with research demonstrating that eclecticism does not work in actual practice the way they imagine. While most professional therapists are eclectic, with the idea that they will use different theories and techniques with different clients for different problems, there is no research proving that they do. In fact, it is our impression, in reading the research and from interviewing one of the leading researchers, that most professional therapists tend to treat the diversity of their clients' problems with the same combination of theories and techniques. The various conferences and workshops where a particular eclectic approach is touted will demonstrate the plethora of problems each eclectic approach is purported to address.

After they attempt to give a positive twist to eclecticism, the Passantinos then say:

This diversity, however, also exposes a serious weakness in the attempt to scientifically validate psychotherapy. If it is classified as a science, it must be *judged* as a science; but if it is subjective and inconsistent, it is not *good* science (36, italics in original).

The Passantinos remind us of a boxer whose opponent is totally open to a possible knockout punch but who only lightly jabs away. Instead of using this statement as one possible disabling punch to psychotherapy, they use it only as a criticism, albeit a serious criticism of psychotherapy as a whole. But do they condemn it totally? NO! As a matter of fact, many practicing psychotherapists have made similar criticisms of the way **other** psychotherapists practice. This permits them, as well as the Passantinos, to deal with the reasons why only **some** professional psychotherapy should be abandoned altogether for Christians. Which therapists by name and which organizations by name are never linked directly with such criticisms. The critics of some psychotherapy who leave the door open to their own psychotherapeutic opinions and practices will not name names of problematic therapists, counseling centers, and clinics, and neither do the Passantinos.

Another criticism used by the Passantinos is the following remark, "Sadly, some counseling does worse than no good at all; it actually *harms* the clients" (36). Here again, an opening for a severe blow to psychotherapy, but the Passantinos say it in one sentence and then quickly pass over it. Any superficial acquaintance with the research will demonstrate that psychotherapy does produce iatrogenic or detrimental effects for many it is intended to help. Instead of a sharp blow at psychotherapy, the Passantinos pull their punch with a brief nod to the existence of harm. And, no name is given to the counseling or organization that harms, because any and all can harm or help, but only according to the Passantinos' formula. We suggest the Passantinos read the chapter titled "Deterioration, Negative Effects, and Estimates of Therapeutic Change" in the *Handbook of Psychotherapy and Behavior Change*, which is regarded as the "bible" of outcome research on psychotherapy (Bergin, 176ff).

The Passantinos end this section by discussing common elements of psychotherapy. But, because of their ignorance, they fail to quote the research that demonstrates that "the training, credentials, and experience of psychotherapists are irrelevant" (Dawes, 62). The common elements in therapy, used by both amateurs and professionals, that contribute to change are common in many kinds of interpersonal relationships and are not dependent on training, credentials, or experience. This section would have been an excellent opportunity for the Passantinos to bring glory to God by pointing out that believers are competent to minister and that professionals have no advantage over them. However, they would never say that because they do not believe it.

"Biblical Counseling"

We find some major problems with this last section, in which they present the Bible as "inadequate" with respect to problems of living. The Passantinos say:

> Christians . . . often focus their criticism on psychotherapy and exhort Christians to return to God's Word for the solutions to their problems. This approach has merit, but it is not only an inaccurate generalization, it also is inadequate (37).

If they believe that exhorting "Christians to return to God's Word for the solutions to their problems" is inadequate, what do they propose? One would agree if they are merely saying that some people need personal ministry, i.e. a coming alongside to minister God's grace, wisdom, and encouragement. However, in this section, they include extrabiblical sources of help. Thus, they appear to suggest that a "return to God's Word for the solutions to their problems" would be inadequate? The bottom line on the Passantinos is they seem to deny the sufficiency of Scripture in dealing with problems of living, and additionally they leave the door open to psychotherapy. Underlying their inadequacy of Scripture position and leaving the door open to psychotherapy is a special theological position that we will discuss later.

The Passantinos have avoided the real problem (the infiltration of psychotherapy into the church) by focusing attention on their own conclusion that the church is to blame for believers seeking psychotherapy. By concentrating on the church's failure, the Passantinos direct attention away from the fact that they leave the door open to psychotherapy and its underlying psychologies, which compounds the church's failure. This is done throughout this article, but strongly in this section. They say:

> We believe that a far more critical concern is the *cause* of this turn away from God's Word to psychotherapy. When the church fails to minister in a complete and biblical way, people's needs go unmet and they turn to other sources for solutions to those needs. The ministry of the church should include support and nurture for its member, including biblical counseling (37, italics in original).

The Passantinos also say:

> When the church fulfills its responsibilities for biblical community, nurture, and support, then Christians will not feel the need to turn to secular psychotherapy. By contrast, as the stories opening this article illustrate, when the church *does not* embrace the repentant alcoholic, the parent with the troubled teen, or those emotionally bruised by sinful behavior, then the hurting and needy will look *elsewhere* for help.
>
> It is our contention that psychotherapy has become enormously popular among Christians primarily because the church has failed to fulfill its biblical obligation to nurture, protect, admonish, and mature its members . . . if psychotherapy offers some help while the local church does not, can we blame those who turn to it for relief? (38).

It is the Passantinos' clear contention that the reason psychotherapy is so successful is because the church has failed. They are partly right, but mostly wrong. The error of the church is that pastors and parishioners have succumbed to the intimidation put forth by mental health organizations, secular psychotherapists, and professional Christian counselors. There was an all-out effort during the 1960s to make pastors feel inadequate in dealing with psychological problems. As a result pastors learned to refer problem-laden people to professional counselors, or they became psychologically trained themselves.

With this intimidation, Christians are afraid to minister without psychological training and therefore they refer people right out of the church into psychotherapy. Along with this intimidation comes a whole host of programs to promote and dispense psychotherapeutic theories and techniques. This is the failure of the church, not the initial inability to minister.

Due to the vast amount of intimidation to which the Passantinos have added, the church has failed to minister, and yet it is still far more successful at dealing with problems of living than psychotherapists. Just think of how much the church could minister if the intimidation were removed or if people truly turned back to the Word of God and trusted Him in ministering to one another in the Body of Christ. Psychotherapists use only their ears to hear and their mouths to speak, but almost never use their hands (except to receive cash, check or credit card) or feet (unless it's to run after those who don't pay) to help, particularly outside the office setting. No therapy or therapist's conversation can compete with the work of the church.

The problem is a multiple one. The church has failed in many ways, but the critical part of the problem is that the door to psychotherapy has been left open by many in the church, including the Passantinos. One of the most flagrant failures of the 20th-century church is the acceptance and promotion of psychology in Christian schools, seminaries, churches, missionary organizations, books, radio, and other media. This repeated false finger pointing at an amorphous church without fingering those various facets of it is dreadful reporting on the part of the Passantinos. If they truly wish to help believers they would specifically name individuals, organizations, and practitioners with unbiblical or unscientific practices. The Passantinos should warn and enlighten rather than to accuse and obscure. By not doing so they have failed the very audience for whom they are writing.

One part of the responsibility must also be placed on the individual. Believers are responsible to do what the Bereans did, i.e. "searched the scriptures daily, whether those things were so" (Acts 17:110). But where do the Passantinos emphasize this?

The Passantinos, appearing not to trust the sufficiency of the Word of God to deal with problems of living, have taken a theological stand that leaves the psychotherapeutic door open. First they blame the church for not ministering and then leave the door open to psychotherapy, which is a major reason why the church is not ministering. Like many psychotherapists, the Passantinos are part of the problem and only provide a compromised solution.

In this final section of Part One, the Passantinos say:

> The term "biblical counseling" is used in different ways by different authors. Some use it to refer to the preaching of God's Word apart from application. Some use it to refer to a counseling approach that "affirms the Bible as its *sole* source for authority concerning human nature, values, and prescriptions for healthy living." Some use the term to refer to counseling that uses the Bible as its foundation and standard, but also borrows compatible and testable information and principles from other sources, such as laboratory experimentation, statistical surveys, clinical experience, and so forth. In this series of articles we use the term in this latter way (37,38).

The source for the inner quote in the above quote refers to John H. Coe and a paper that he presented to the International Christian Association for Psychological Studies. While most readers have not heard of Coe, it is important to note that it is really Coe's theology that the Passantinos are promoting.

Notice within this paragraph the openness to "clinical experience." What is clinical experience? Clinical is in contrast to experimental. Clinical psychologists are those who therapize patients. Apparently the Passantinos are leaving the door open to a psychotherapist's self-evaluation as a basis for judgment. If they mean something other than that, they should clarify, because information gained from clinical experience is highly individual and subjective.

With respect to the term *biblical counseling*, the Passantinos say, "Some use the term to refer to counseling that uses the Bible as its foundation and standard, but also borrows compatible and testable information and principles from other sources." The phrase "borrows compatible and testable information and principles from other sources" is explained and then the Passantinos naively state, "When we use the principles of God's Word as our standard (2 Tim 2:16), and we understand how to evaluate claims (2 Tim 4:2), we can confidently test the truth or falsity of a claim" (38). That statement sounds as if it came right from the American Association of Christian Counselors (AACC), which is an association of integrationists (those who use psychology **and** the Scriptures).

Gary Collins, president of AACC, makes the following statement, which is widely endorsed by Christian psychologists:

> When a psychologist seeks to be guided by the Holy Spirit, is committed to serving Christ faithfully, is growing in his or her knowledge of the Scriptures, is well aware of the facts and conclusions of psychology, and is willing to evaluate psychological ideas in the light of biblical teaching—then you can trust the psychologist, even though he or she at times will make mistakes, as we all do. If the psychology or psychological technique is not at odds with scriptural teaching, then it is likely to be trustworthy,

especially if it also is supported by scientific data (Collins, 19).

If one were to ask the numerous Christian psychologists if they meet Collins' criteria, they would all say they do. But then we have to ask, why it is that these numerous Christian psychologists, who would say that they meet Collins' criteria, come to contradictory conclusions about what therapeutic systems to use and which techniques to apply? There must be a lot of proof-texting, to say the least.

There is a great need for dealing with the issue of what is and what is not compatible with Scripture. There are numerous claims about compatibility with Scripture. For example, psychiatrists Frank Minirth and Paul Meier claim that all the Freudian ego-defense mechanisms are found in Scripture. There are many examples of what various psychotherapists have attempted to support with Scripture, including the Freudian Oedipus complex. We challenge the Passantinos to find one Christian psychologist who will state that what he is practicing is incompatible with Scripture. In spite of the great variety of the sometimes contradictory approaches of Christian therapists and the fact that many of these approaches have extremely unbiblical foundations, we have never found a practicing Christian therapist who confessed that what he is doing is unbiblical. It is obviously easy to biblicize any of the psychotherapeutic approaches, no matter how silly or satanic they might be. How sad that the Passantinos took such little time to explore this important and complex issue rather than expressing their personal opinion undergirded by the work of Coe.

In the following paragraph the Passantinos parrot John Coe's views, when they say:

Our presupposition is that God works authoritatively and infallibly in His written Word, but also dynamically in the world and among people. While we look to God's Word as the standard by which to judge all things (1 Thes 5:21,22), we recognize that the same God who preserved His Word also gave the world order and consistency, created natural laws, created humans with the ability to use logic and reasoning processes to apply biblical principles to new situations and to understand new experiences, and gave us the ability to develop testing tools to help us understand ourselves and the world around us (38).

The Passantinos expand on Coe's psychotheology in Part Two. Therefore we will critique their psychotheology in more detail in our response to Part Two.

The subtitle of Part One of this four-part series on psychology is titled "Laying a Foundation for Discernment." It should actually be titled "Laying a Foundation for Deception." The Passantinos, by expressing their biases under the guise of objective reporting on psychology and by leaving the door open to psychotherapy and its underlying psychologies, have established a doorway of deception through which many Christians will walk.

2

Responding to Part Two

"The 'Biblical Counseling' Alternative"

We are responding only to the last section of Part Two, because there were few flagrant problems in the preliminary sections. However, lumping us together with the biblical counseling movement (BCM) is a major faux pas on the part of the Passantinos, since we had preceded their series by over a year with our book titled *Against Biblical Counseling: For the Bible*. We should have been referred to as critics of the BCM.

The Passantinos use a number of logical fallacies throughout their four articles. In this last section of Part Two the Passantinos demonstrate their knowledge and use of the straw man fallacy. A logic text states:

The *straw man* fallacy occurs when an arguer responds to an opponent's argument by misrepresenting it in a manner that makes it appear more vulnerable than it really is, proceeds to attack that argument, and implies that he or she has defeated the opponent. It is called the straw man fallacy because, rather than attacking the "real man," the opponent sets up and knocks over a "straw man" (Johnson, 260).

Instead of dealing with the real BCM, the Passantinos have set up a straw BCM so they can appear to be attacking the real BCM.

"Inadequacies of the BCM"

First "inadequacy":
The first inadequacy mentioned by the Passantinos is as follows:

> First, the BCM generally fails to recognize that some of what we learn about God, ourselves, our relationship to God, and our relationships to others comes from what are called *natural theology* (understanding God and His relationship with the universe by means of rational reflection) and *general revelation* (that which can be known about God generally—especially through the created world—on a universal basis) (28, italics in original).

Note the phrase, "fails to recognize that some of what we learn." The first inadequacy of the BCM stated by the Passantinos is an inadequacy on their part. We were a part of the BCM for 20 years, wrote about it, spoke at conferences and corresponded with many of its leaders over the years, and we would say that the Passantinos invented this inadequacy to support their psychotheology. Depending on what the Passantinos mean by what they say, we know of no one in the BCM who "fails to recognize" those things mentioned in the above quote. However, those in the BCM would also recognize the severe limitations of natural theology and the real purpose of general revelation.

The Passantinos say:

> God speaks not only specially (in the Bible, through prophets, and in His Son—*see* Hebrews 1:1-2), but also through reason, the material universe, social history, and conscience (28).

We know of no one in the BCM who would deny that some things can be discovered by these natural means. The very basic issue, however, is whether such humanly discovered truths can be properly categorized as "revelation," either general or specific. The Passantino criticism proceeds upon the assumption that the theological category "general revelation" (or, as is often used synonymously, "natural theology") is composed of all such humanly discerned truth-claims. They find support for this proposition in the writing of John Coe, a faculty member of Rosemead School of Psychology. It would be appropriate to say that the Passantinos have used Coe's theology to support their presuppositions about psychology.

If one accepts the theology of Coe as explained by the Passantinos, one would conclude just what the Passantinos concluded, even though they have misrepresented the BCM position in their first-mentioned inadequacy. However, Doug Bookman, a professor at The Master's College, has written a paper presenting a refutation of Coe's position and therefore the Passantinos' theological position.

Because we are attempting to be brief in our response, we will quote sparingly from the Bookman paper. Bookman reveals "three primary and fatal flaws" in Coe's theology viz. his epistemology, anthropology, and bibliology.

Epistemology is defined as "the study or theory of the origin, nature, methods, and limits of knowledge." In describing Coe's position, Bookman says, Coe "regards the claim that the Bible alone is sufficient as a source of spiritual/moral knowledge as 'comically and tragically' mistaken" (Bookman, "In Defense of Biblical Counseling," 5). In concluding his discussion of Coe's position, Bookman says:

> I have suggested that this proposition is flawed in that it commits the basic error of natural theology, assuming that there is a world of metaphysical truth outside of Scripture which can be discovered by the unaided efforts of men (Bookman, "In Defense of Biblical Counseling," 9).

In another place, Bookman makes the case that the rationale employed by Coe and others in defense of such an epistemology is dangerously flawed. Very briefly, that rationale is accomplished by an arbitrary and unbiblical broadening of the definition of *general revelation*.

General revelation is an important theological concept. Conservative theologians have used the term *general revelation* to identify a very narrow category of truth that God has made powerfully evident (thus the word *revelation*) to every rational human being (thus the word *general*), according to the way He fashioned the moral and physical universe. Romans 1 and 2, the most important New Testament discussion of general revelation, states unequivocally that the revelation God has set before all men, through the infinitely mysterious, complicated physical universe and through the moral consciousness of all human beings, renders all humans without excuse when they reject that truth.

Lately, however, the important theological category of general revelation has been broadened to include all truth-claims made as a result of human efforts to understand the many aspects of the created order. Those who have broadened the category argue that the Scriptures are indeed the "special" revelation which God has left to us and that, because God is the Author of the entire created order, whenever men discover "truth" in that order, we can refer to that humanly discovered "truth" as "general revelation."

Bookman identifies the very dangerous ramifications of the argument that replaces the biblical doctrine of general revelation.

> First . . . by defining general revelation as that body of truth which is gained by human investigation and discovery, the argument is guilty of neglecting the element of non-discoverability which is intrinsic to the biblical notion of revelation and supplanting that notion with its exact antithesis. Further, the approach is dangerous in that it attributes to the truth-claims of men an authority which they do not and cannot possess, and renders it virtually impossible to bring those truth-claims under the authority of the one standard by which God demands that they be measured.
>
> Second, the argument . . . is confused in its definition of the term "general." By mistakenly taking that term to refer to the *content* of the category (rather than to the *audience* to which the revelation thus denominated is available), the apologists who employ this argument commit two fallacies which are destructive of orthodox theology: first, they expand the category to include all manner of truth-

claims which have no right to be thus honored; and second, they eviscerate the character of revelation by including in the category truth-claims which are admittedly lesser than the truths of Scripture, which demand that finite and fallen men measure them to determine their validity, and which at best can *possibly* issue in a higher level of insight into the demands of living (Bookman, "General Revelation," 10, italics in original).

Bookman concludes that:

. . . as described in Scripture, general revelation is truth which is manifestly set forth before all men (Rom 1: 17-19; 2:14,15); it is truth so clear and irrefutable as to be known intuitively by all rational men (Ps 19:1-6; Rom 1: 19); it is truth so authoritative and manifest that when men, by reason of willful rebellion, reject that truth, they do so at the cost of their own eternal damnation (Rom 1:20; 2:1,15). For this seamless, flawless and majestic tapestry of God-given truth is substituted a patchwork of "lesser" truths, of truth which "is obtainable at least in part," truths which "are not delineated for us by God" but are "discovered by fallible humans" . . . . Surely such a concept of general revelation represents a ravaging of the biblical concept (Bookman, "General Revelation," 9).

Anthropology. Coe quite clearly denies the effect of sin upon the fallen mind of man. Bookman identifies as absolutely basic to Coe's argument the proposition that "fallen man retains the ability and propensity to deduce truth from the created world and thus to arrive at conclusions which are as authoritative as the Scriptures themselves" (Bookman, "In Defense of Biblical Counseling," 15).

Coe defends such a proposition, not by any exegetical consideration of relevant biblical passages, but rather by pointing out that the sage in the book of Proverbs explicitly says he learned some things by observing the natural order and that those things are recorded in Scripture. Coe concludes that if it could be done by the biblical sage, it can be done by any human being. However, such a parallel is illegitimate. The conclusions drawn from the supposed parallel are wrong and dangerous.

More central to the issue of biblical anthropology, however, is that Coe's argument involves a denial of the biblical insistence that divine truth is foolishness to the natural man (1 Cor 2:14), that apart from regeneration man's understanding is darkened and alienated from the life of God (Eph 4:17), that all men are enemies in their minds until God transforms them through the work of salvation (Col 1:13), and that from the sole of the foot even unto the head there is no soundness in fallen man (Isa 1:5). Further, even regenerated man is crippled by the continuing corruption of sin, as well as by the reality of his own finiteness (Isa 55:8,9; 1 Cor 2:16). Thus, for any man, saved or lost, to suppose that his thoughts ought to be regarded as certain and/or as authoritative as those of God—let alone the notion that all human truth-claims deserve such respect, simply because the sage of the Old Testament sometimes related his articulation of truth to observations he had made in the natural order— is to deny what the Bible says so often and so clearly about the real fallenness and finiteness of man and about the infinite wisdom and matchless authority of God.

Bibliology. Bookman says:

> Coe's purpose in developing [his] argument from the Wisdom literature is to insist that "the scriptures recognize a non-propositional source of wisdom embedded and evident within the patterns and

dynamic structures of both the inorganic and organic world" . . . he is convinced that the knowledge possessed by the sage and recorded by him in Scripture was discovered by the sage alone, with no dependence upon God (Bookman, "In Defense of Biblical Counseling," 15,16).

Bookman summarizes:

The point of all this is that Coe has drawn a wholly unwarranted conclusion when, on the basis of the OT sage's supposed "discovery" of moral truths, he deduces the legitimacy of a "science" of values, derived from contemporary investigation into the supposedly "normative" world of nature. Coe's perceived parallel between the *ministry* of the OT sage and the *work* of the modern social scientist simply does not exist (Bookman, "In Defense of Biblical Counseling," 22,23, italics in original).

Bookman gives one additional summary:

The issue here relates very directly to the character of inspired Scripture. Wisdom literature, such as that which is represented by the sage in the book of Proverbs, is one of many precious and profitable genres of biblical literature. But the recorded message of the sage, no less than that of the prophet, the Gospelist or the writer of a New Testament epistle, is authoritative and dependable *simply and only because it was breathed out by God* (2 Tim 3:16). The prophets received their messages by means of dreams (Num 12:6); that doesn't suggest that the dreams of men today are just as authoritative as those of the prophets. The sage normally received his message by means of observation; it is erroneous to conclude that therefore the observations of any man are as authoritative and/or dependable as those observations of the sage *which are recorded in the pages of sacred Scripture*. Note carefully that the debate here is not whether any of the observations made by human beings might be true. Rather, the debate is whether the observations of men today ought to be regarded as possessing the absolute certainty and/or normative authority which the Bible possesses in all of its parts. The words of the sage are not certain and authoritative *because* they were discovered by observation, any more than the words of Jude are certain and authoritative *because* he cites them from the apocryphal book of Enoch (Jude 14). The words of all biblical writers are authoritative because the recording of them was done under the careful supervision of the Holy Spirit which is known as "inspiration." To regard the words of men as possessing the same sublime dignity and ultimate authority that the words of the Bible possess is remarkably dangerous (Bookman correspondence, italics in original).

The Passantinos' understanding of general revelation is all-encompassing but erroneous. In one fell swoop they even reduce sections of Scripture to less than God-breathed in their attempt to show that God's revelation refers to that which can be discovered through observation and natural reason. The word *revelation* refers to an unveiling, a revealing of something that could not be otherwise discovered or known. What mankind gleans through observation, reason and logic is not revelation, but discovery. These discoveries can be very helpful to mankind, such as the discovery of electricity. The kind of psychology the Passantinos are both criticizing and defending may include some discovery about the superficial aspects of man through observation, reason and logic, but these kinds of theories include highly subjective, speculative imaginations about the depths of man.

Regarding Coe's psychotheology, Dave Hunt says:

> In order to justify "Christian" psychology's borrowing of the "wisdom of this world" (1 Cor 1:20;2:6;3:19) from Freud, Jung, et al. and calling it part of "God's truth" to supplement the Bible, [Coe] must show that the Bible is insufficient—or abandon his profession.

Hunt further says:

> Coe claims that the Bible itself "mandates the church to develop a science of [moral and spiritual] values and human nature" from extrabiblical sources. He declares that whatever is "natural" is good and that one can deduce a "science of [moral] values" simply from observing nature. This is obviously not true.
>
> Nature has no morals; nor can science reveal morals; neither can there be a science of human nature because man is not a robot and human qualities such as love, joy, peace, choice, a sense of right and wrong, etc. cannot be explained in scientific cause-and-effect terms. Einstein confessed that science has nothing to do with religion; and Nobel Laureate physicist Erwin Schroedinger said that science "knows nothing of . . . good or bad, God and eternity." Mankind's common recognition of right and wrong comes not from nature but from God's laws written in the conscience (Rom 2:14-15). Moreover, nothing is more "natural" than to eat the fruit of a tree, especially if it is delicious and promises the knowledge of good and evil!

Regarding Coe's article, Hunt says:

Coe accuses those who affirm the sufficiency of Scripture of having "retreated, particularly from the light of reason and natural revelation, to the island of faith, clinging desperately and unfortunately to the illusion of a Bible-alone approach to wisdom which is solely 'from above.'" He sounds like a humanist! He declares that without natural revelation "the Bible . . . alone is insufficient." Of course, he includes in natural revelation that part of "God's truth" which secular psychologists have allegedly discovered and which is therefore needed to supplement Scripture.

Yes, the Bible is insufficient when it comes to flying an airplane, repairing an engine, transplanting a kidney, but not when it comes to those "things that pertain to life and godliness," *all* of which Peter says have been given to us in Christ (2 Pt 1: 3-4). Paul says that through Scripture alone the man or woman of God is "throughly furnished unto all good works" (2 Tm 3:17). Christ said that the Holy Spirit is "the Spirit of truth, *whom the world cannot receive*" (Jn 14:17) and who guides believers "into all truth" (Jn 16:13). He said that those who continue in His word, which "is truth" (Jn 17:17) know "*the* truth" (Jn 8:32), not part of the truth, and are thereby set *free,* not partially free.

The Bible's declaration that the "natural man" cannot know God's truth, which is only revealed by the Spirit of God (1 Cor 2:14), is proof that Freud, et al. had nothing of God's truth to impart. That fact alone thoroughly demolishes the Coe/Christian psychology thesis that part of God's truth is to be found in secular psychology. It isn't there.

Inasmuch as all of God's truth is contained in God's Word, Christian psychology has nothing to offer and leads into gross error. Preventing God's people from believing in the sufficiency of Scripture is essential for Christian psychologists if they hope to remain in business, and John H. Coe is determined to prove this thesis (Hunt, Q & A, re Coe).

Second "inadequacy":
The Passantinos present what they perceive to be a second inadequacy of the BCM. They say:

> Second, since the BCM fails to recognize varieties of God's communication to humans in natural theology and general revelation, it also establishes a false standard of comprehensive exclusivity regarding the Bible. The BCM wrongly assumes that the Bible is the sole source of all values and prescriptions, when in reality *God is*, and the Bible is *one of the ways* God communicates the values and prescriptions (28, italics in original).

Notice how this second so-called BCM inadequacy is dependent on the Coe/Passantino psychotheology. What many in BCM fail to do is agree with the Coe/Passantino version of general revelation. Instead, BCM advocates do recognize that any form of natural theology is severely weakened and distorted by the noetic effects of the Fall.

Bookman summarizes this facet of Coe's thesis as follows:

> Objective Source of Values Thesis: There exists an objective extra-biblical source of values and wisdom in the patterns and dynamic structures of nature, particularly in human phenomena, which can be discovered by human observation and reflection. . . .

Coe argues that there exists an objective, empirically knowable and demonstrable source of ultimate metaphysical reality outside of special revelation (Bookman, "In Defense of Biblical Counseling," 1-2).

What Coe does not apparently realize is that what may be seen and reflected upon is severely limited by the unsearchable depths of the inner person and the inability of fallen man to observe objectively, without the intrusion of sinful biases. We who trust the Bible as sufficient for life and godliness say that the Bible is the sole authoritative source of understanding the human condition, including values, and sole authoritative source of prescribing how one is to live. None of the humanly derived observations or strategies can ever be regarded as possessing certainty or authority equal to that of Scripture.

The BCM position is confidence in the unique authority and thus the full sufficiency of Scripture. Such a regard for the character and authority of Scripture comes from an exegetical consideration of those Scriptures themselves, because the Bible claims to be the very Word of God (2 Tim 3:16; 2 Pet 1:21, et al.) and it sets itself infinitely above the words of men (Ps 19:7-11; 119:160).

But the Passantinos call into question the very possibility of drawing such conclusions upon the basis of interpreting Scripture. They ask, "how do counselees know that the interpretation and/or application of Scripture given them by their BCM counselor is accurate?" (28). To answer that question we ask a counter question: How do the Passantinos know that their use of "reason, the material universe, social history, and conscience" is accurate? In the area of "values and prescriptions," regarding the inner man (volition, cognition, emotion, purpose, conscience, etc.), would the reader rather trust Scriptures or "reason, the material universe, social history, and conscience"?

The Passantinos say, "God uses other people, personal observation, rational discourse, experience, and, as we have already seen, natural and general revelation *as well as* the Bible" (28, italics in original). However, "people, personal observation, rational discourse [and] experience" are all distorted because of the Fall. There are serious problems in attempting to use general revelation to support integrating secular psychological theories and therapies with the Bible to help Christians live more effective lives. Through such integrated counseling, psychological systems intrude into the believers' process of sanctification or Christian living. One must remember that the more than 400 different systems of psychotherapy were devised by nonChristians. One must wonder how the subjective notions of unbelievers about the depths of man have been elevated to such a high status in terms of understanding the human condition and prescribing how Christians should change and live.

We have dealt with this important subject of general revelation and how it relates to secular psychological theories and therapies in our book *The End of "Christian Psychology"* (Bobgan, Ch 3).

It is difficult to justify the idea that those who rejected the very existence of God can know either the character of God or the human soul through general revelation. Cornelius Van Til put it this way:

> After sin has entered the world, no one of himself knows nature aright, and no one knows the souls of man aright. How then could man reason from nature to nature's God and get anything but a distorted notion of God? The sort of natural theology that the sinner who does not recognize himself as a sinner makes is portrayed to us in the first chapter of Romans (Van Til, 69).

Notice the indictment on mankind found in Romans 1. After properly perceiving truth about God through nature, people consistently suppress that truth. Therefore, one wonders how psychological theorists, such as Freud, Jung, Maslow, Rogers, and Ellis, who have suppressed the truth about God, can now dip into general revelation about humans, who were created in the image of God. Romans 1 clearly states that those who rejected God "became vain in their imaginations, and their foolish heart was darkened. Professing themselves to be wise, they became fools." By rejecting God's revelation of Himself they have forfeited the ability to gain accurate self-knowledge or a true understanding of the inner person through such general revelation.

God has revealed His "eternal power and Godhead" through Creation, but one must have His special revelation to know the "breadth, and length, and depth, and height" (Eph 3:18) and to "know the love of Christ, which passeth knowledge" (Eph 3:19). God has already revealed in His Word who man is and how God is known and how man is to grow in the spirit. "All scripture is given by inspiration of God, and is profitable for doctrine, for reproof, for correction, for instruction in righteousness: That the man of God may be perfect, thoroughly furnished unto all good works" (2 Tim 3:16,17). There is no psychotherapeutic system that can even approach that goal.

While general revelation confronts all men with very limited truth about God, those who want to justify using psychology see Scripture as giving only general ideas about man and thus needing to be supplemented with specifics. Consequently, they appeal to what they think is included in general revelation to discover specific details about the human mind, will, emotions, and behavior to fill in what they believe is missing from the Bible. They trust the opinions of unsaved individuals to explain the details of the soul on the basis of their view of general revelation.

God in His common grace does allow unbelievers to investigate His universe and discover physical laws, but such discoveries do not deserve the title "revelation," nor are they worthy of the measure of certainty with which men ought to regard a word directly from God (which is precisely what *all* revelation is). Further, there is a huge difference between understanding aerodynamics, for instance, and knowing the complexities of the human soul. While superficialities can be observed about mankind, the depths of human nature elude scientific investigation and morality is beyond its comprehension. Natural reason can draw some conclusions from observation, but these again are at the superficial level and subject to human distortion. Anything beyond the superficial ends up being speculation and opinion.

Scripture is clear about who is able to know and understand the inner man. "The heart is deceitful above all things, and desperately wicked: who can know it? I the LORD search the heart, I try the reins, even to give every man according to his ways, and according to the fruit of his doings" (Jer 17:9). Knowing the inner workings of the human heart, soul, mind, and spirit is God's domain. Because He is the primary Person molding each of His children who have been born again by His Spirit, this is His prerogative to know and to reveal.

While people may learn very general things about human nature through observation, it is presumptuous to assume specificities gleaned from such psychotherapeutic theorists as Freud, Jung, Maslow, Rogers, Ellis, and others were revealed by God. Natural man can only know about the most superficial aspects of man. The deeper one plunges into man, the more he needs God's special revelation about the inner man. Psychology cannot deal with man's sinful nature or God's remedy for sin and provision for spiritual growth. At best, psychology can only give wild guesses about the most important aspects of man. It is here where only God's Word can be trusted.

Just as general revelation does not show the way of salvation, general revelation cannot give any information about the new life in Christ or about sanctification or Christian growth. At best, psychological theories and therapies are limited to helping the old nature or flesh. They cannot touch the "new man, which after God is created in righteousness and true holiness" (Eph 4:24). Scripture is clear about unbelievers having their "understanding darkened, being alienated from the life of God through the ignorance that is in them, because of the blindness of their heart" (Eph 4:18). Therefore it is pointless for Christians to attempt to improve their psyche (soul) through psychology or to look to the wisdom of men for how to live.

The "wisdom of psychology" is the very wisdom of men about which God warns: "That your faith should not stand in the wisdom of men, but in the power of God" (1 Cor 2:5). Those of us who believe Christians should not integrate secular counseling psychologies with the Bible are often dismissed with such shibboleths as "all truth is God's truth," when, in fact, the kind of psychology we are opposed to is made up of opinions and myths, rather than truth. Which of the more than 400 different psychotherapeutic systems (which disenfranchise each other at least to some extent) or the 10,000-plus techniques (many of which contradict each other) can be considered to be God's truth as revealed through general revelation? These do not constitute God's truth. They are "science falsely so called." Christians should follow Paul's admonition to Timothy: "O Timothy, keep that which is committed to thy trust, avoiding profane and vain babblings, and oppositions of science falsely so called: Which some professing have erred concerning the faith" (1 Tim 6:20,21).

When one considers all the admonitions in Scripture regarding foolish speculations, why would God give special insights regarding the innermost mysteries of the soul to those who have denied Him? Paul clearly presents God's position regarding the wisdom of men:

> For it is written, I will destroy the wisdom of the wise, and will bring to nothing the understanding of the prudent. Where is the wise? where is the scribe? where is the disputer of this world? hath not God made foolish the wisdom of this world? . . . Because the foolishness of God is wiser than men; and the weakness of God is stronger than men. . . . But God hath chosen the foolish things of the world to confound the wise. . . . That no flesh should glory in his presence. But of him are ye in Christ Jesus, who of God is made unto us wisdom, and righteousness, and sanctification, and redemption (1 Cor 1:19, 20,25,27,29,30).

> But the natural man receiveth not the things of the Spirit of God: for they are foolishness unto him: neither can he know them, because they are spiritually discerned. But he that is spiritual judgeth all things, yet he himself is judged of no man. For who hath known the mind of the Lord, that he may instruct him? But we have the mind of Christ (1 Cor 2:14-16).

Paul further warned the Colossians: "Beware lest any man spoil you through philosophy and vain deceit, after the tradition of men, after the rudiments of the world, and not after Christ" (Col 2:8).

Third "inadequacy":
Armed with an erroneous psychology and theology, the Passantinos blunder into the third so-called error of the BCM. They say:

> The third fundamental inadequacy of the BCM is that it presents a falsely restrictive and dichotomized view of science and faith, and, consequently, of human nature and of the parameters of psychology as science (29).

The Passantinos claim:

> The BCM view of science is adopted from a non-Christian Enlightenment philosophy of science that wrongly divorced material realities from immaterial realities and wrongly affirmed empiricism (knowledge gained through sense verification) in isolation from other tools of knowing (29).

The Passantinos are apparently not aware that there are eminent philosophers of science who have examined this area of science and examined the differences between the material and the empirical and would be in opposition to the two individuals the Passantinos quote as authorities in this section.

Sir Karl Popper, who is considered by some to be the greatest philosopher of science of our time, has investigated the differences between physical theories, such as Newton's theory of gravity and Einstein's theory of relativity, and theories about human behavior. He began to suspect that the psychologies underlying the psychotherapies could not truly be considered scientific. After researching these differences and examining the theories formulated by Freud, Adler and others, Popper concluded that those theories, "though posing as sciences, had in fact more in common with primitive myths than with science; that they resembled astrology rather than astronomy" (Popper, 343). As many have demonstrated, psychotherapy is not a coherent science, but rather a discipline based on many unscientific theories and few verifiable facts.

In their confusion about God's revelation and the ability He has given mankind to discover things about His created universe and in their added confusion between His revelation and His sovereignty, the Passantinos say:

> The BCM advocates, in their zeal to preserve the supremacy of the Bible as God's sole revelation, have actually *limited* God's supremacy by agreeing with the secular humanists that one can "know" material *reality* apart from God (29, italics in original).

Another false accusation. BCM advocates do not limit God's supremacy by distinguishing between revelation and discovery and between revelation and metaphysical speculation. Every BCM person we know believes in God's supremacy over His entire universe. They believe that God has created mankind with abilities to discover things about the universe and that much can still be discovered even though all mankind suffers from the noetic effects of the Fall. And, they further believe that all good gifts come from God and that He is sovereign over all. The Coe/Passantino version of general revelation actually limits God's special revelation as given in His Word.

Reasoning like the Passantinos, we could rewrite the above paragraph to read as follows:

> The [Passantinos], in their zeal to [restrict] the supremacy of the Bible as God's [special] revelation, have actually [expanded] God's [general revelation]

by agreeing with the [New Agers] that one can "know" [the immaterial depths of man] apart from God.

One writer on the New Age says:

> It is significant to remember that the present New Age movement has its origins in the counterculture of the sixties and early seventies. Early inspiration came from the writings of Abraham Maslow, Eric Fromm, Rollo May, Carl Rogers, and others. This generation of psychologists was the first to reject scientific materialism as the basis of the study of human existence (O'Hara, 371-372).

Again, reasoning like the Passantinos, we could then say that the view that the Passantinos are advocating sounds like a New Age view. The New Age view obliterates or obscures the line between mind and matter, between the tangible and intangible, between the body and the spirit, and between a material and immaterial universe. This psychotheology of Coe and the Passantinos would certainly have great appeal to the New Ager.

Then in the same paragraph, as a contrast to their false representation of the BCM position, the Passantinos say:

> The thoughtful Christian [obviously in contrast to the BCM person], however, recognizes that one cannot divorce God's presence from any successful pursuit of truth because God's sovereignty extends throughout all reality, material, and immaterial (29).

We know of no BCM person who would not recognize "that one cannot divorce God's presence from any successful pursuit of truth because God's sovereignty extends throughout all reality, material, and immaterial." One does not have to reduce God's general revelation to human discovery and speculation to believe that "God's sovereignty extends throughout all reality, material, and immaterial." Through His wisdom and goodness, God has allowed mankind to discover a limited amount of knowledge about the universe, and He has given His Word to reveal the depths of the inner man.

The result of all the Passantinos' razzle-dazzle about science and faith and the physical and spiritual is found in what they say in the following:

> When BCM counselors approve a godless medical doctor but not a godless psychologist, they are promoting the same "scientism" that has excluded God from science. They are saying that empirical science can safely make judgments about physical conditions, but not about nonmaterial or spiritual ones. The Christian should understand that humans are not essentially physical nor essentially spiritual, but instead are both physical and spiritual, the two natures creatively knit together in one rational person created in the image of God (30).

The Passantinos pursue their new-age-like view of a physical and spiritual continuum. Their treatment of the two as one continuum for empirical science to "safely make judgments about" is simplistic and violates a number of logical and scientific parameters.

If you go to a doctor when you're physically sick, what's wrong with seeing a psychologist for mental-emotional-behavioral problems? That question is asked by those who confuse the use of medicine with the practice of psychotherapy. Individuals making such an error assume that the medical and the mental can be thought of and talked about in the same manner and with the same terms. This error is one of using the medical model to justify the use of psychotherapy which involves a false analogy.

In the medical model physical symptoms are caused by some pathogenic agent. For example, a fever may be caused by viruses; remove the pathogenic agent and you remove the symptom. Or, a person may have a broken leg; set the leg properly and the leg will heal. People have confidence in the medical model because it has worked well in the treatment of physical ailments. With the easy transfer of the model from medicine to psychotherapy, many people erroneously believe that mental problems can be thought of in the same way as physical problems.

Dr. Ronald Leifer, in his book *In the Name of Mental Health*, says:

> If we grant that in . . . medicine the term "disease" refers to the body, to modify it with the word "mental" is at worst a mixture of logical levels called a category error, and at best it is a radical redefinition of the word "disease." A category error is an error in the use of language that, in turn, produces errors in thinking. . . . Whatever the mind may be, it is not a thing like muscles, bones, and blood (Leifer, 36-37).

Leifer discusses the arguments for the medical model and then the defects of such arguments. He concludes by saying:

> The principal advantages of this argument are therefore neither scientific nor intellectual. They are social. They prejudice the lay public to see psychiatric practices as more like medical treatment than like social control, socialization, education, and religious consolation. It bids them to presume that the

psychiatrist, like other physicians, always serves the individual in his pursuit of life, health, and happiness (Leifer, 38).

The use of the medical model in psychotherapy does not reveal truth; instead it merely disguises psychotherapy with the mask of medical terminology and ends up confusing everyone. Research psychiatrist Torrey says:

> The medical model of human behavior, when carried to its logical conclusions, is both nonsensical and nonfunctional. It doesn't answer the questions which are asked of it, it doesn't provide good service, and it leads to a stream of absurdities worthy of a Roman circus (Torrey, 24).

Using the medical model of human behavior and confusing medical with mental through a false analogy can lead to justifying support for ESP, past lives, UFOs, Eastern religions, and the occult. Transpersonal or religious psychologies are being supported through such false analogies and usage of the medical model.

While the Passantinos' blurring, if not removing, the line between the physical and spiritual is a delight to the New Ager and would be a consternation to Popper and other philosophers of science, it raises all kinds of questions about their knowledge in this area and their competence to deal with this subject.

Fourth "inadequacy":
The Passantinos say:

> Finally, because the BCM wrongly limits godly wisdom to the Bible alone, it easily can neglect to nurture client-specific effective communication and application of godly principles. The BCM counselor

who truly held Scripture as the exclusive source of godly wisdom would merely repeat Scriptures without personal intervention or interpretation (30).

A footnote at the end of the first sentence in the above quote refers the reader to the Passantinos' third article in the series. Therefore we will not comment on it here. However the second sentence involves a logical fallacy.

To expose this fallacy, we substitute the word *pastor* for "BCM counselor." The sentence now reads: "The pastor who truly held Scripture as the exclusive source of godly wisdom would merely repeat Scriptures without personal intervention or interpretation." Sounds like the slippery slope fallacy to us, because the first part of the sentence does not necessarily lead to the claimed result in the second part. The pastor or the BCM counselor can truly hold to Scripture "as the exclusive source of godly wisdom" and not be confined to "repeat Scriptures" only. Preachers, teachers, and evangelists are not confined to either repeating only Scripture or appealing to the Passantinos' non-material, intangible, unprovable, subjective, so-called science of psychotherapy and its underlying psychologies. If that's what they are saying, then they have committed the either-or logical fallacy, which gives only two possibilities, such as one must either quote Scripture in counseling or use "natural and general" wisdom.

The Passantinos end this part by saying:

> However, its inadequacies, especially in the area of wrongly isolating God's sovereignty from some fields of study and practice, should encourage modification of current biblical counseling approaches toward a more comprehensive godly counseling movement (30).

Those who look to the Bible for God's truth are not "wrongly isolating God's sovereignty from some fields of study and practice." As stated earlier, they believe in God's sovereignty in all areas of endeavor, but they also recognize the difference between the wisdom of God and the wisdom of men.

The Passantinos are committed to leaving the door open to their psychotheology and to encouraging its use in the church. While we have written about some ungodly aspects of the biblical counseling movement, we would be opposed to the Passantinos' idea of a "more comprehensive godly counseling movement" based on their psychotheology borrowed from Coe.

Footnote:
There is a footnote (#4) at the end of Part Two that we were going to ignore. However it is such a good example of how subtleties often elude the Passantinos that we decided to address it.

In the footnote the Passantinos speak of some BCM advocates who "make contradictory remarks." Then they immediately say:

> For example, Martin and Deidre Bobgan universally describe psychotherapy negatively in their book *Psychoheresy* in such statements as, "The theories of psychological counseling poison the soul" (7); "Psychological theories and methods continue to subvert Christianity" (23); "The research results [in this book] also call for an elimination of the cure of minds (psychological counseling) in all of its forms, no matter where it exists in the church and no matter how popular and talented the psychologizers" (56); and "Psychotherapy intrudes upon some of the most important themes of Scripture. . . . To dress these [theories and techniques] up in biblical termi-

nology and call them Christian is to compound the evil" (12). However, in a subsequent book, *Prophets of Psychoheresy II* (Santa Barbara, CA: EastGate Publishers, 1990), the Bobgans accused us (the Passantinos) of misrepresentation for referring to Martin as "representing the position that all psychotherapy is evil and unbiblical" (274). They protested, "We have never made such a statement! It was contrived by the Passantinos, attributed to us, and is a misrepresentation" (274). Regardless of some proponents' inconsistent and scattered exceptions to their condemnations, the BCM as a whole rejects all psychotherapy and usually rejects most general psychology as well (30).

They are obviously referring to us as making "contradictory remarks" and believe that the above quotations from us prove them right. Unfortunately for them the above quotations prove just the opposite.

The only quote of ours that contains the word *evil* is the following: "To dress these [theories and techniques] up in biblical terminology and call them Christian is to compound the evil." Neither this sentence or the others quoted prove that our position is "that all psychotherapy is evil and unbiblical." To say that psychotherapy is an evil in the church is not the same as saying that "all psychotherapy is evil and unbiblical." An example may suffice. If we were writing about Mormonism instead of psychotherapy we would have said, "To dress [Mormonism] up in biblical terminology and call [it] Christian is to compound the evil." The Passantinos would have accused us as "representing the position that all [of Mormonism] is evil and unbiblical," which we would not say. We do condemn psychotherapy when used by Christians, but we have never said, "All psychotherapy is evil and unbiblical." After all, even a broken clock is correct twice a day, but you wouldn't want to tell time by it. One would think the Passantinos would be able to understand something that simple.

3

Responding to Part Three

"Can Psychology Be Integrated with Christianity?"

According to the Passantinos, the answer to the question raised by the title of Part Three is "yes," but only if one will follow the formulas they offer. The Passantinos believe that, if one pays careful attention to what they say, one will be able to skirt around all the land mines of errors associated with the use of secular psychology and be able to use it. The Passantinos give two models for their formula, viz. Dr. William Backus and Dr. James Dobson. Their recommendation contradicts what they have said earlier in this series and demonstrates clearly that what the Passantinos recommend cannot be accomplished.

The Passantinos begin this part by mentioning a "national professional psychotherapy convention." They draw six conclusions from their experience. We will only comment on the first and last of these conclusions. They say, "First, almost everyone we talked to had a genuine concern for people with problems and an earnest desire to devote their lives to helping others" (16). We would not comment on this if they had said "seemed to have" instead of "had." We have attended numerous workshops, classes, conferences and talks by psychotherapists. As writers we have also been at such meetings with secular humanists, New Agers, and even occultists. We have never been to a one of these meetings where we could not say what the Passantinos had said about the psychotherapy convention, except we would have to replace "had" with "seemed to have."

There are usually sessions at these professional psychotherapy conventions on "Niche markets to increase your revenues," "Drop-in groups for singles at $5 a head so the group members will enroll for individual psychotherapy greatly increasing your monthly income," "Infertility is much more than a medical problem—it is a source for new clients," etc. This lack of discernment on their part has led to their overlooking the possible motives of those at the convention and results in a missed opportunity to reveal the variety of reasons attendees are at such a meeting. Many are there to learn how to better commercialize what they do. Others want to reinforce what they are already doing. Some to learn how to avoid lawsuits. Yet, many others are there to learn new approaches to attract and help more clients. But, many are at such conferences to learn how to maintain their incomes in the era of managed care. And, the Passantinos may have missed the fact that many are there to learn about new spiritualities or to expand on their present ones.

The final conclusion they list from having attended the convention is:

And sixth, we learned firsthand that anyone who pronounces a universal blessing or a universal condemnation on psychotherapy has failed to understand its complexity and diversity (16).

It is interesting what the Passantinos learned "first hand" from all of what they refer to as "genuine," "devoted" psychotherapists at the convention.

It may be that the Passantinos know someone "who pronounces a universal blessing . . . on psychotherapy." We repeat, therefore, that we have been to numerous workshops, classes, conferences, and talks and do not know of one person "who pronounces a universal blessing . . . on psychotherapy." We have spoken and corresponded with numerous supporters and opponents of our point of view, but we have not found such a person as described by the Passantinos. Even the avid supporters with whom we speak would not pronounce a "universal blessing . . . on psychotherapy." We recently spoke with a university professor who is also a practicing clinical psychologist. He is an avid supporter of **his** brand of psychotherapy, but he would never pronounce "a universal blessing" on psychotherapy. We challenge the Passantinos to identify even one of their oft-quoted integrationists who would pronounce "a universal blessing on psychotherapy."

On the other hand a number of individuals do pronounce a "universal condemnation on psychotherapy." According to the Passantinos such individuals "failed to understand its complexity and diversity." If you, like us, have this point of view, you need not worry. You are in excellent company, because there are many eminent philosophers of science, historians of psychotherapy, psychotherapy researchers, and theologians who would disagree with many of the Passantinos conclusions. It is not that these eminent individuals fail "to understand its complexity and diversity"; they understand the complexity and diversity far more than the Passantinos. For example, licensed psychologist Dr. Tana Dineen, in her book *Manufacturing Victims*, says:

> Unfortunately, in the 90's, it has become the accepted role of psychologists to categorize people in these debilitating ways and to turn them into victims and, thus, patients. Adopting the same arrogant tone which so disturbed me back in the 70's, psychologists now translate all of life into a myriad of abuses, addictions and traumas. And they do this not only in psychiatric hospitals and psychology offices but in homes, schools, business settings, media interviews and in courtroom testimony everywhere. It has become the accepted practice to substitute personal belief and theoretical dogma for scientific fact. Psychologists are claiming to know what is "good" and what is "bad," what hurts people and what helps them, and their answers are making people unsure of themselves and suspicious of each other. Psychologists are striving to promote and extend their influence at the expense of creating a society which is self-absorbed and distrustful. By authoritatively defining which human actions and feelings are to be encouraged and which are not to be tolerated, they are dictating how men and women are to live their lives and how society is to function (Dineen, 12).

Dr. Thomas Szasz, who as mentioned earlier is probably one of the most distinguished psychiatrists in the world and who has a long list of life-time distinctions, in speaking of what psychotherapy has done to religion, contends:

... contrition, confession, prayer, faith, inner resolution, and countless other elements are expropriated and renamed as psychotherapy; whereas certain observances, rituals, taboos, and other elements of religion are demeaned and destroyed as the symptoms of neurotic or psychotic illnesses (Szasz, *Myth of Psychotherapy*, 188).

Referring to the replacement of the biblical with the psychological, Szasz says:

Educated in the classics, Freud and the early Freudians remolded these images into, and renamed them as, medical diseases and treatments. This metamorphosis has been widely acclaimed in the modern world as an epoch-making scientific discovery. Alas, it is, in fact, only the clever and cynical destruction of the spirituality of man, and its replacement by a positivistic "science of the mind" (Szasz, *Myth of Psychotherapy*, 104,105).

It is not only a matter of the "destruction of the spirituality of man," but a destruction of religion itself. Szasz further contends that psychotherapy "is not merely indifferent to religion, it is implacably hostile to it" (Szasz, 27-28).

The universal blessing/universal condemnation quote illustrates a method the Passantinos appear to use to their advantage. They state two positions as extremes and then end up being the ones to take the seeming middle road, thereby communicating the idea that both "extreme" positions are in error and that their position is the reasonable one. This leaves the impression that those of us who oppose psychotherapy are simply extremists and thereby wrong. This approach in the pursuit of truth is certainly no virtue on their part.

What the Passantinos are saying in essence is that those who pronounce "a universal condemnation on psychotherapy," regardless of how knowledgeable they are in science or theology, have "failed to understand its [psychotherapy's] complexity and diversity." Apparently the Passantinos would have us believe that irrespective of educational background, accomplishments, writings, extensive research, and distinctions, such individuals have "failed to understand its [psychotherapy's] complexity and diversity." Common sense would dictate that one would know enough not to make such an accusation.

"Psychology and Psychotherapy"

This section repeats some of what was already said in Part One. Therefore the reader can review our response to Part One, which covers the major concerns about this section.

"History of Psychotherapy"

The Passantinos mention "Two frustrating problems psychotherapy advocates face." They say:

> The first problem involves success rates . . . most of the comprehensive data available on the effectiveness of psychotherapy shows that its success is much more modest that most people have assumed. . . . The second frustration is that research has been unable to support the superiority of one school of therapy over another (19).

When one adds these two "frustrations" to the fact of negative effects of psychotherapy and the fact that psychotherapy is not science and the fact that amateurs do as well at psychotherapy as professionals (Dawes, 15) to all the other facts that would be "frustrations" to therapists, one would think the Passantinos would lead the reader to a logical conclusion of closing the door on psychotherapy. But that is **not** what they do.

They begin the final paragraph of this section by saying:

> A Christian who attempts to use psychology within a framework of biblical principles for personal counseling faces unique challenges and a myriad of pitfalls (19).

However, following this warning, the Passantinos describe how to be a better therapist. And, to confirm their pro-psychotherapy position, they end this section with a quote from Stanton Jones and Richard Butman. Who are Jones and Butman? They are two supporters of an open door to psychotherapy for Christians. The Passantinos, like Jones and Butman, have a preconceived commitment to an open door to psychotherapy—under certain conditions, of course.

In giving their advice, the Passantinos say, "Such a Christian must be *better* prepared in theology, biblical interpretation, and principles of Christian discipleship than he is in psychology" (19, italics in original). This is one of the numerous disagreements we have with the Passantinos' articles. A Christian who is "prepared in theology, biblical interpretation, and principles of Christian discipleship" is thereby prepared to minister and can be used by the Holy Spirit to do so—period! The Christian does not need and would be less effective learning and using the theories and techniques of psychology. And, we would challenge the Passantinos to demonstrate from the research that learning and using the theories and techniques of psychotherapy, even under the conditions they set, would be of any added help to the Christian. Their inability to do so should be a wake-up call to them as well as others in the integrationist camp.

This section is more evidence of the Passantinos' inadequacy of Scripture position. To put it bluntly, God's people have never needed the help of psychotherapy and they are much better without it until His return.

"Foundations of Contemporary Psychologies"

The Passantinos begin this section by identifying branches of psychotherapy. They say:

> Three main branches of psychotherapy have provided the foundation for the myriad of contemporary psychotherapeutic techniques, theories, and assumptions: dynamic psychologies, behavioral psychologies, and humanistic psychologies (19).

While different authors group psychotherapies in various ways, we subscribe to four branches instead of three. The fourth branch is the existential or transpersonal branch. Although Maslow is regarded as a key promoter of humanistic psychology, he believed that it was merely a stepping stone to transpersonal or spiritual psychologies. He predicted a move from centering in self to centering in the cosmos, from self-transformation to spiritual transformation. He wrote:

> I consider Humanistic, Third Force Psychology to be transitional. A preparation for a *still higher* Fourth Psychology, transpersonal, transhuman, centered in the cosmos rather than in human needs and inter-

ests, going beyond humanness, identity, self-actualization and the like (Maslow, iii-iv).

Through such transpersonal psychotherapies, various forms of Eastern religion are creeping into Western life. Psychologist Daniel Goleman quotes Chogyam Trungpa as saying, "Buddhism will come to the West as psychology." Goleman points out that Asian religions "seem to be making gradual headway as psychologies, not as religions" (84). It is a serious failure on the part of the Passantinos not to cover this branch of psychotherapy as there are many Christians being therapized by these Eastern religions (absent their origins) through their psychotherapeutic clones.

Following their introduction to this section, the Passantinos give an elementary textbook summary of the three branches of psychotherapy. While there are several problems in their three subsections, we will only comment on three errors of fact.

In the "Dynamic Psychologies" subsection, the Passantinos say, "Most psychodynamic therapies last a long time (such as twice-weekly 50-minute sessions for three to five years)" (20). However, the *Handbook of Psychotherapy and Behavior Change* reveals:

> There has . . . been a dramatic change in the way that psychodynamic psychotherapy is practiced today. It has become much more eclectic, **abbreviated**, and specifically targeted. The therapy has become **short term** and **focused** (Bergin, 824, bold added)

It is doubtful that "Most psychodynamic therapies last a long time" any more, especially under new managed care restrictions.

The Passantinos begin the "Behavioral Psychologies" subsection by stating:

> The second building block of contemporary psychotherapy was the development of behaviorism, first by Freud's disciple Alfred Adler, and then under academic psychologist John Watson (21).

We have read, studied, taught, and written on Adler over the years. However, we have never read of Adler being one of the first behaviorists or even a behaviorist at all. To check this out, we called the North American Society of Adlerian Psychology (NASAP). They were equally puzzled. It may be that Jones and Butman, the source of this information, know more about Adler than those in NASAP. The fact is that one can turn any of the early theorists into a behaviorist. One can even twist Freud into a behaviorist. If the Passantinos would like, we will demonstrate how. But it certainly would confuse the streams of psychotherapy and definitely muddy the already murky waters. The fact that cognitive-behavior theorists have combined some of Adler's ideas with behaviorism does not make Adler a behaviorist. It simply shows how easy it is to mix the streams and further muddy the waters. The Passantinos inclusion of the Jones-Butman view of Adler tells more about the Passantinos' unnecessary dependence on Jones and Butman than about Adler.

The Passantinos' third error is in the "Humanistic Psychologies" subsection. They say, "Transactional Analysis (TA), developed by Eric Berne, is one of the most popular forms of humanistic psychology" (22). TA was very popular in the 60s and early 70s, but to say that TA "is one of the most popular forms of humanistic psychology" today is erroneous. In the late 70s we surveyed members of the Christian Association for Psychological Studies (CAPS). CAPS is an organization of psychologists who are professing Christians. We asked which therapeutic approaches most influenced them. The results indicated that TA was not "one of the most popular" ones. The Christian psychotherapeutic practitioners reflect quite readily their secular psychotherapeutic counterparts.

In the last of the subsections, the Passantinos discuss what they call "'Seat-of-the-Pants' or Pragmatic Psychotherapy." They use this section to discuss eclecticism as a prologue to their next major section, which includes a chart. It is rather amusing to see them rightfully criticizing eclecticism and those who wrongfully use it as a fanfare for their own solutions to the problems. The simple solution is to condemn all psychotherapy for Christians, to recommend avoiding it altogether, and to encourage a restoration to mutual care in the Body of Christ. After all, what did the church do without psychotherapy for almost 2000 years?

In this subsection, the Passantinos state that "some Christian psychologists have attempted to develop a good system in their 'integration' discussions" (23). In the footnote related to this comment, they refer to "Gary Collins," "Meier et al.," "Benner," and "Jones and Butman." We would say that none of them has developed a "good system in their 'integration' discussions," but they all think they have. Here again we challenge the Passantinos to find any integrationists who would say that they have **not** "attempted to develop a good system in their 'integration' discussions."

The Passantinos then say:

> The most popular contemporary Christian psychologists, such as James Dobson, Gary Collins, Frank Minirth, Paul Meier, Fred Gross, and William Backus, come under particular scrutiny in these areas. Each criticism does not apply to each therapist, nor always to the same degree. Nonetheless,

too frequently they do not explain what underlying comprehensive biblical world view they may possess; they promote techniques and/or ideas for which they do not demonstrate a clear biblical compatibility; and they fail to explain that they have redefined common terminology to fit their world views (23).

Instead of using this opportunity to link each person named with a specific criticism, the Passantinos string out the six names of the "popular contemporary Christian psychologists" and criticisms in such a way that not one of them can be tied to any one criticism. There is no way the reader can determine from the article if any one of the individuals is mildly guilty, moderately guilty, or severely guilty, and thus it is difficult to attach any guilt to any one of them. Leading to even further absolution of these "popular contemporary Christian psychologists" is the fact that two of the six (Backus and Dobson) are later held up as quintessential models of what the Passantinos are recommending and all but one is favorably quoted.

After criticizing eclecticism, the Passantinos say:

> Eclecticism is not completely useless, especially for the Christian who can build from other systems a quasi-system that more or less reflects the broad approach of the Bible to personal development (23).

They end the subsection with a quote from two integrationists who say:

> So, as the Christian therapist moves beyond a secular theory, one needed area of growth is an expanded vision of technique that incorporates the eclecticism found in Scripture (23).

They do not explain what they mean by *eclecticism* in Scripture, which leads the reader to equate eclecticism in psychotherapy with the Bible, as if these are somehow equal.

This section confirms again that the Passantinos leave the door open to psychotherapy in spite of its radical weaknesses. The Passantinos' views are highly compatible with the integrationist views of Stanton Jones and Richard Butman, authors they depended on for this series.

Another person quoted favorably by the Passantinos is psychologist Paul Vitz. Vitz should be a prime target of Passantinos' criticisms for his views on psychology. Vitz has said, "Oedipal motivation is a reasonably apt characterization of original sin." Vitz concludes that "Jesus is the anti-Oedipus" (Vitz, 4). One only needs to have a superficial understanding of Freud's Oedipal theory to know how erroneous and even blasphemous such statements are. There is plenty to specifically criticize in the case of all the integrationists quoted favorably by the Passantinos, including Jones and Butman. The Passantinos' lack in this area is a great disservice to the church and further evidence of their predilections for psychotherapy.

"Special Problems With Christian 'Integration'"

As a part of a summary, the Passantinos say:

> For Christian "therapy" (counseling) to be truly helpful and biblically based, it must start from the firm biblical foundation of a Christian world view, with each technique part of a coherent biblical paradigm (24).

They say, "Thoughtful Christians with both theological and psychological competence" need "a contextual definition to explain how psychology and the Bible could intersect. (The above chart clarifies some of the assumption problems in integrating common psychotherapy ideas with Christian beliefs)" (23). The Passantinos' chart lists six areas of concern with the supposed "secular" and "Christian" responses. The greatest problem with the chart is that it does not do what it's supposed to do, viz. clarify "some of the assumption problems in integrating common psychotherapy ideas with Christian beliefs." To begin with, the comments about secular psychotherapy are not universally true. One comment in the "Secular" column is "Religion is irrelevant." This is far from being universally true among secular psychotherapists. Many secular psychotherapists have a religious orientation, though not Christian. Additionally there are many secular psychotherapists who have great regard for their client's belief system and who are committed to understanding and dealing with it in therapy. The Passantinos should have become aware of this at the "professional psychotherapy convention" they attended.

The comments in the "Christian" psychotherapy column distinguish no one and do not lead to a resolution of the problems with psychotherapy that the Passantinos raise. The Christian psychotherapists would agree with each statement in the list and particularly affirm the last one: "Uses biblical standards, rejects contrary ones, accepts complementary ones." Since those who consider themselves Christian psychotherapists would see this list as already describing themselves, no change or improvement would be accomplished by this chart.

Also, the psychotherapists would be most agreeable with the Passantinos' statement that:

Most Christian psychologists will agree that integration *cannot* include any compromise of a biblical world view, theology, or doctrines of humanity, sin, and redemption. They would say that responsible integration must *exclude* compromise, omission, or contradiction of biblical theology (23,24, italics in original).

To support their own position, the Passantinos then give two lengthy quotes by Gary Collins and William Backus. Both quotes can be used to support an integrationist view that is compatible with the Passantinos. But this rhetoric is not realized in practice, not because of lack of intention to do so by Christian psychotherapists, but rather because all believe they are "clean" and that only others are not. The reason why none of the practitioners will "name names" of either individuals or organizations who should be criticized or elevated as examples of excellence is because what is idealized about psychotherapy cannot be realized. It cannot be realized because of what psychotherapy truly is and not what it pretends to be. And, to incriminate others may lead to self incrimination.

The lack of scientific and theological support for psychotherapy is sounding a death knell for psychotherapy, but few in the church are listening. The Passantinos' suggestions and recommendations to safely integrate psychotherapy are naive and idealistic. The ship of psychotherapy is scientifically and theologically scuttled and the Passantinos are doing their utmost to save it from sinking into oblivion.

The Passantinos say:

It is not possible to embrace wholeheartedly any one of the three foundational schools without compromising one's Christian world view or becoming hopelessly inconsistent (24).

We would change that sentence for the purpose of demonstrating the extreme differences we have with the Passantinos by removing a few words as follows:

> It is not possible to embrace . . . any one of the . . . schools without compromising one's Christian world view or becoming hopelessly inconsistent.

However, it is not just a few words that separate our conclusions from those of the Passantinos, but rather a vast number of scientific and theological volumes.

"The Bottom Line for the Christian"

In this last section the Passantinos present a number of their conclusions, such as:

> [Psychology] can't be summarily embraced or dismissed (24).

> None of these assumptions [from the "major kinds of psychologies"] is compatible with a comprehensive Christian world view (24).

> Christians risk practicing biblically inconsistent counseling when they fail to adhere closely to an underlying coherent biblical world view (24).

While some of what they report sounds contradictory, the overall message of this section supports the open door to psychotherapy.

The Passantinos present the integrationist views of two authors when they say:

> . . . it is at least logically possible to affirm that "a Christian psychotherapist can *within limits* practice any one of many counseling techniques and approaches; and may choose. . . to use several methods, depending on his skills and the particular problems of his clientele" (24, italics and ellipsis in original).

The Passantinos then confirm their own integrationist view by stating their conditions:

> . . . first, the Christian therapist's understanding of and commitment to a comprehensive, coherent, biblical world view; second, an understanding of the foundations of the various psychologies; third, an examination of how integrally any theory or technique is connected to its foundational psychology; and fourth, an assessment of the degree of correspondence that can be obtained between a given theory or technique and biblical principles (24).

Since all Christian psychotherapists would consider that they already meet those conditions, the Passantinos are not only leaving the door wide open; they are unwittingly inviting Christians to trust all Christian therapists because they would all claim to meet those conditions.

In contrast to the Passantinos' integrationist view, our position is that the Bible alone is sufficient to deal with the issues and problems of living No one needs to add psychological training. The Passantinos' insufficiency-of-Scripture position is very evident in this section and is similar to that of many of the integrationists they quote.

In one brief paragraph in the previous section, the Passantinos sound critical and name some psychologists, but then compromise what they say. In this section they finally are complimentary and specific. They say:

Among the myriad of practices and ideas, however, Christians may attempt to discern helpful therapies compatible with a Christian world view. For example, Dr. William Backus has borrowed and redefined aspects of cognitive therapy into a counseling system that focuses on helping clients to conform their thoughts to Christian truth, and then have their "Christianized" thoughts conform their behavior; Dr. James Dobson, who does not have a clinical practice, frequently mentions the importance of "self-esteem," but he has attempted to redefine the term within the Christian context of God's love for us as His creations, and the sacrificial love He expressed toward us "while we were still sinners" (Rom. 5:8) (24).

We assume that, since these are the only two favorable examples in this four-part series, they represent the best the Passantinos could come up with. If these fail the test, then so have the Passantinos failed with respect to their open door to psychotherapy rationale. Let's take a look at the two prime positive examples of William Backus and James Dobson to see if the Passantinos' ideas work in practice.

The Passantinos in Praise of Backus. The popular Christian book *Telling Yourself the Truth* by Dr. William Backus, a clinical psychologist, and Marie Chapian, a psychotherapist, is one of the many examples of exaggerated, unfulfilled promises in Christian books. The book utilizes cognitive therapy, particularly from Albert Ellis's Rational Emotive Behavior Therapy (REBT),[*] along with

---

[*] Formerly Rational Emotive Therapy. For an analysis of Albert Ellis's Rational Emotive Behavior Therapy, see our book *The End of "Christian Psychology,"* Chap. 13.

some biblical ideas. The front cover of the book promises that you will: "Find your way out of depression, anxiety, fear, anger and other common problems by applying the principles of misbelief therapy." The authors state:

> Misbelief therapy will work for you. It will work for you even if nothing else has because its effectiveness depends upon very explicit psychological laws which are as universal as the law of gravity (25).

This is a universal promise that supposedly empowers the process (Misbelief Therapy) as if it were omnipotent over "depression, anxiety, fear, anger and other common problems." Like the "law of gravity" it will supposedly cause cure no matter what. Common sense would dictate that if such promises were true everyone would be using misbelief therapy, whereas it is only one of a myriad of approaches used by therapists. In Part One we quoted the *Handbook*'s repeated conclusion of "The Equal Outcomes Phenomenon." In addition, no independent research or follow up studies exist to prove the phenomenal promises of that system. Yet, this book is supposed to help **other** people tell themselves the truth.

In Part One the Passantinos refer to "scientific objectivity and testing one would expect from a practitioner of a science" (Part One, 36). However, they completely ignore their statement when it comes to Backus. The *Handbook* reveals that REBT is "the least adequately tested of all the major approaches" (Bergin, 458). By their own standards, the Passantinos should be criticizing Backus, not complimenting him.

Earlier in Part Three, the Passantinos assert that "the core of behaviorism (including rational emotive therapy), with its assumptions of strict naturalism, determinism, and physicalism, is completely incompatible with Christianity" (21). It is clear that William Backus is steeped in the use of Rational Emotive Behavior Therapy (REBT). As we noted, Backus believes that his cognitive approach, which is based on REBT, follows so-called psychological laws. Backus claims that "its effectiveness depends upon very explicit psychological laws which are as universal as the law of gravity." We recommend *Think on These Things* by Debbie Dewart, which exposes the unbiblical roots and practices of Backus and others.

The promises in *Telling Yourself the Truth* are erroneously supported by misunderstanding and misapplying Scripture. Backus and Chapian use Proverbs 23:7, "For as he thinketh in his heart, so is he," to promote their inflated promises and prescriptions "to help you possess the happiness you desire and to be the person you'd like to be" so that "You can live happily ever after with the person you are and make a profound affect on those around you because of it" (10). However, the full context of that verse says that one should not go solely on outward appearances.

> Eat thou not the bread of him that hath an evil eye, neither desire thou his dainty meats: For as he thinketh in his heart, so is he: Eat and drink, saith he to thee; but his heart is not with thee. The morsel which thou hast eaten shalt thou vomit up, and lose thy sweet words (Prov. 23:6-8).

The "he" referred to in Proverbs 23:7 is a person not to be trusted. The proverb is a warning to watch out for duplicity. Proverbs 23:7 cannot be used to teach that if a person changes his thoughts he will possess the happiness he desires or will become the person he would like to be. Nor can it be used to support the idea that one will "live happily ever after" if he practices misbelief therapy. When anyone begins with psychology and attempts to use

Scripture to support an idea, he is likely to end up both misunderstanding and misapplying Scripture.

The book includes a great deal of self-talk that has to do with notions from humanistic psychology as well as Scripture. There is enough Scripture to make these new beliefs sound biblical, but the reason for self-talk comes from the notion that one must develop positive self regard. Just as in secular cognitive therapy, the person is encouraged to see himself as a person of worth and to rescript his life with positive statements about himself. Just as with secular cognitive therapy, the beliefs that must be replaced are those that devalue the self, the circumstances, or the "prospects for the future" (39). Negative self talk is to be replaced with positive self talk.

An entire chapter is devoted to dealing with self hate, which is not addressed in Scripture, since Scripture teaches that people do, indeed, love themselves, even though they may hate the discrepancy between who they are and what they would like to be. As in Ellis's REBT, Backus's misbelief therapy aims to help a person have a better self-image and to have good opinions about self that are not dependent on other people's opinions. Typical of the advice given in this integrative approach is: "You can't honor your neighbor as he ought to be if you don't give honor to yourself" (105). This is, of course, dependent on a misinterpretation of the Great Commandment and teaches that one can't love God and neighbor until one learns to love oneself.

Two **misbeliefs** identified with one poor soul who supposedly hated himself are: "It is more Christian to please other people than to please myself," and, "It is wrong not to be willing to forget my own wants to please friends and family when they want me to." Note that these are identified by Backus and Chapian as *misbeliefs*. Yet, we have to ask, are these beliefs always wrong? Aren't there times when these are right attitudes and pleasing to the Lord? The most important person to please is the Lord, Himself. Then people don't have to talk themselves into pleasing themselves instead of other people.

Here is what Backus and Chapian say about what Scripture teaches:

1. Our life, including our opinions, feelings, wants and needs, is not less valuable or important than anyone else's needs and
2. Our life, including our opinions, feelings, wants and needs, is not more valuable or important than anyone else's (107).

While the second of the two statements is closer to the Bible than the first, the above teaching comes right out of Ellis's REBT. Scripture teaches that we are to esteem others better than self (Phil 2:3). Moreover, both of the above statements are false, because some opinions, if they are based on Scripture and fact, are more important than other opinions, no matter who makes them. And, some people's needs are greater and therefore more important than the needs of others. However, this kind of self-talk is typical of cognitive therapy.

Many more examples could be given from Backus's brand of integration to show that this example of Christians blending psychotherapy and Christianity fails to meet the criteria on the Passantinos' chart on at least two counts: "Truth" and "Techniques." According to the Passantinos' own words, there is a contradiction between their condemnation of "the core of behaviorism (including rational emotive therapy)" and their praise of Backus, who is a prime popular user of it. This contradiction requires explanation. It is paradoxical that the Passantinos would recommend someone as a model who is practicing and recommending an approach they have already condemned.

In reference to the Passantinos' recommendations, Backus may intend to have a "comprehensive, coherent, biblical world view," but it is not evident in the presentation of his integration. If he wants to help people live by the truth, he should stick with the Bible rather than combine God's Word with Ellis's REBT. If Backus has "an understanding of the foundations of the various psychologies" and conducted "an examination of how integrally any theory or technique is connected to its foundational psychology," he should have known enough to avoid attempting to merge Ellis with the Bible.

Ellis is an avowed atheist who repeatedly through his writings insists that faith in God is an "irrational Belief." Ellis declares, "The very essence of most organized religions is the performance of masochistic, guilt-soothing rituals, by which the religious individual gives himself permission to enjoy life." He continues, "Religiosity, to a large degree, essentially is masochism; and both are forms of mental sickness" (Ellis, "The Case Against Religion," 6). Ellis declares:

> If one of the requisites for emotional health is acceptance of uncertainty, then religion is obviously the unhealthiest state imaginable: since its prime reason for being is to enable the religionist to believe in a mystical certainty (Ellis, "The Case Against Religion," 6).

Ellis believes that faith in God is not based on reality, but on fantasy. He says about the human condition:

> One of his highly human, and utterly fallible, traits is that he has the ability to fantasize about, and to strongly believe in, all kinds of nonhuman entities

and powers such as devils, demons, and hells, on the one hand, and angels, gods, and heavens, on the other hand (Ellis, *Humanistic Psychotherapy*, 2).

He responds to reports about people benefiting from religion by saying:

> REBT acknowledges that a belief in religion, God, mysticism, Pollyannaism, and irrationality may at times help people. But it also points out that such beliefs often do much more harm than good and block a more fully functioning life (Ellis, *Reason and Emotion*, 387).

As for the Passantinos' fourth recommendation of assessing "the degree of correspondence that can be obtained between a given theory or technique and biblical principles," Backus has to twist Scripture to make it correspond with Ellis's cognitive theory and technique. One does not need cognitive theory or therapy to determine how one's beliefs are to change. That is already in Scripture. Moreover the Bible does more than present truth. It is active and alive. It does far more than any human system could ever do.

> For the word of God is quick, and powerful, and sharper than any twoedged sword, piercing even to the dividing asunder of soul and spirit, and of the joints and marrow, and is a discerner of the thoughts and intents of the heart. Neither is there any creature that is not manifest in his sight: but all things are naked and opened unto the eyes of him with whom we have to do" (Heb 4:12,13).

It is amazing and tragic to see what people have chosen to follow instead of or in addition to the Lord and His living Word.

The Passantinos in Praise of Dobson. James Dobson is a leading promoter of self-esteem in the church. We wrote a book about him entitled *Prophets of PsychoHeresy II*. A section in one of the chapters is titled "Bob and Gretchen Passantino: Witch Hunters?" In it we say, "Bob and Gretchen Passantino are a good example of how devotion to an individual such as Dobson can influence thinking, conclusions, and even accusations" (269). We should have referred to a devotion to an integrationist position, which includes James Dobson, William Backus, Gary Collins, Stanton Jones, Richard Butman, and others.

Although the Passantinos contend that Dobson "has attempted to redefine the term" *self-esteem* (24), Dobson uses the word in much the same way as psychologists who are not Christians. The main difference with Dobson is that he attempts to make Scripture support his self-esteem ideas and he teaches that people can get their self-esteem from God. The Passantinos' use of Romans 5:8[*] to defend Dobson's use of "the importance of 'self-esteem'" is exemplary of how far they are willing to go to defend him. Dobson evidently believes that salvation is a reason for self esteem. He says:

> . . . what greater source of self-esteem can there be than to know that Jesus would have died for him if he were the only human being on earth (Dobson, "Little Ones. . . ," 5).

---

[*] "But God commendeth his love toward us, in that, while we were yet sinners, Christ died for us" (Rom 5:8).

But, should salvation cause a person to esteem himself?

When one considers why Jesus had to die to save sinners, there is no room for self-esteem. Paul describes every unsaved person's horrible condition as "alienated and enemies in your mind by wicked works" (Col 1:21), "dead in trespasses and sins," "children of disobedience," "fulfilling the desires of the flesh and of the mind," and "children of wrath" (Eph 2:1-3). Then Paul declares, "But God, who is rich in mercy, for his great love wherewith he loved us, even when we were dead in sins, hath quickened us together with Christ (by grace ye are saved)" (Eph 2:4-5). Salvation rests on God's abounding grace, not on personal worth.

Dr. Trevor Craigen questions the doctrine of redemption being used "to proclaim that man is something worth dying for, and that one may now attribute to himself dignity, worth and significance or may see himself as something worthwhile." He says:

> In Scripture no context presenting the wonder and grandeur of salvation even remotely suggests or attempts to apply the doctrine in such a way so that anyone may now validly conclude himself to be worth dying for, or himself to be worthwhile and significant. . . . Salvation is, in all of its aspects, a testimony of the grace of God toward those who were unworthy of eternal life and of His love. Salvation signifies, not the worth of man, but the sinfulness of man (Craigen, 43).

The Bible says that Jesus died to save sinners. He saved us because of our sin and utter depravity, not because of our goodness, value, and worth. The Bible says, "Christ died for the ungodly" (Rom 5:6). Even children need to be taught a proper biblical view of the goodness of God and the depravity of man. And, to set up a hypothetical situation, that "Jesus would have died for him if he were the only human being on earth," is to depart from Scripture and to indulge in speculation. Even if that were so, it would not give just cause for self-esteem. Instead, it would show forth the mystery of God's mercy and grace.

The foundational meaning of the word *grace* is unmerited favor. How can we be saved by grace and not that of ourselves (Eph 2:8) if we are of independent value and worth? If we are of value and worth in ourselves, then it is not grace. It is a business transaction. If we are of intrinsic value and worth, Jesus' death was not a sacrifice but a shrewd bargain. Whenever we move from the mercy and grace of God in terms of salvation and put independent value on ourselves, we are saying that people deserve to be saved, because they are worth it, or people deserve to be loved by God, because they are lovable and worth His love.

Our book on Dobson demonstrates clearly that his use of self-esteem is compatible with secularists and is incompatible with the Bible. The concept of self-esteem dominates his work. Self-esteem, with its entourage of other self-hyphenated words, permeates his teaching. It began in his first book, came to full bloom in his second book, and serves as a major presupposition throughout the rest of his writing and speaking. *In Dare to Discipline* he says:

> Self-esteem is the most fragile attribute in human nature; it can be damaged by a very minor incident and its reconstruction is often difficult to engineer (Dobson, *Dare to Discipline*, 19).

The major theme and purpose of Dobson's book *Hide or Seek: How to Build Self-Esteem in Your Child* is increasing self-esteem. He says:

It has been my purpose to formulate a well-defined philosophy—an approach to child rearing—which will contribute to self-esteem from infancy onward (Dobson, *Hide or Seek*, 58,59).

One of Dobson's primary objectives for *What Wives Wish Their Husbands Knew about Women* is to: "Point the pathway toward greater self-esteem and acceptance" (Dobson, *What Wives Wish*, 14).

For Dobson self-esteem, self-worth, self-acceptance and their related self-words are crucial, not only for the individual but for the society as well. He contends that "low self-esteem is a threat to the entire human family, affecting children, adolescents, the elderly, all socioeconomic levels of society, and each race and ethnic culture" (Dobson, *What Wives Wish*, 24). As with most promoters of self-esteem, Dobson equates low self-esteem with feelings of inadequacy, inferiority, self-doubt, and an inadequate sense of personal worth.

He continues his litany of woe for a society which does not do all it can to increase personal worth and self-esteem. He says:

The matter of personal worth is not only the concern of those who lack it. In a real sense, the health of an entire society depends on the ease with which its individual members can gain personal acceptance. *Thus, whenever the keys to self-esteem are seemingly out of reach for a large percentage of the people, as in the twentieth-century America, then widespread "mental illness," neuroticism, hatred, alcoholism, drug abuse, violence, and social disorder will certainly occur. Personal worth is not something human beings are free to take or leave. We must have it, and when it is unattainable, everybody suffers* (Dobson, *Hide or Seek*, 2,italics in original).

He contends that social problems are the direct result of people unsuccessfully trying to deal with inferiority or feelings of self-doubt. He has even named a law after himself. "Dobson's Law" says:

> When the incidence of self-doubt is greatest, accompanied by the unavailability of acceptable solutions, then the probability of irresistible social disorder is maximized (Dobson, *Hide or Seek*, 160).

Dobson further declares, "Inferiority even motivates wars and international politics." In fact, he attributes the attempted genocide of the Jews in Germany to an inferiority complex (Dobson, *Hide or Seek*, 165).

Things get reversed when discussing inferiority. Suddenly, the most egotistical people are excused with a diagnosis of inferiority. It begins to sound like Isaiah's prophecy:

> Woe unto them that call evil good, and good evil; that put darkness for light and light for darkness; that put bitter for sweet, and sweet for bitter. Woe unto them that are wise in their own eyes, and prudent in their own sight (Is 5:20-21).

Not only that, Dobson declares that inferiority feelings are "the major force behind the rampaging incidence of rape today" (Dobson, *Hide or Seek*, 166). Thus he contends that low self-esteem is the cause of all kinds of problems, and high self-esteem is an absolute necessity for survival. The issue of self-esteem is not a peripheral issue with Dobson. It is central to all he teaches about children, adults, and society. It is such a foundational assumption for him that it permeates all of his other work.

Self-esteem is a highly popular concept. The California legislature passed a bill creating the California Task Force to Promote Self-Esteem and Personal and Social Responsibility. The legislature funded the bill with $245,000 a year for three years, for a total of $735,000.

The Mission Statement of the Task Force is stated in its Annual Progress Report as follows:

> Seek to determine whether self-esteem, and personal and social responsibility are the keys to unlocking the secrets of healthy human development so that we can get to the roots of and develop effective solutions for major social problems and to develop and provide for every Californian the latest knowledge and practices regarding the significance of self-esteem, and personal and social responsibility (California Task Force to Promote Self-Esteem and Personal and Social Responsibility, "1987 Annual Report to the Governor and the Legislature," v).

Like Dobson, the Task Force believed that esteeming oneself and growing in self-esteem will reduce "dramatically the epidemic levels of social problems we currently face."

As evidence of the identification between Dobson's self-esteem position and the Task Force is the fact that Dobson was featured in their *Esteem* publication. Considering how few people were featured over the three-year period and the fact that Dobson was one of them speaks volumes. In addition, Dobson was listed in the Task Force publication *Self-Esteem Curricular Resources, Books and Other Resources*. We called the Task Force office and asked if Dobson objected to being featured in the *Esteem* publication or listed in the resource publication and we were told "no."

To investigate the relationship between self-esteem and social problems the state Task Force hired eight professors from the University of California to examine the research on self-esteem as it relates to the six following areas:

1. Crime, violence and recidivism.
2. Alcohol and drug abuse.
3. Welfare dependency.
4. Teenage pregnancy.
5. Child and spousal abuse.
6. Children failing to learn in school.

Seven of the professors researched the above areas and the eighth professor summarized the results. The results were then published in a book titled *The Social Importance of Self-Esteem*. Dr. Neil Smelser, the professor who summarized the research admitted the following:

> One of the disappointing aspects of every chapter in this volume . . . is how low the associations between self-esteem and its consequences are in research to date (Mecca et al., 15).

David L. Kirk, syndicated writer for the *San Francisco Examiner*, after examining *The Social Importance of Self-Esteem*, says it more bluntly:

> Those social scientists looked hard . . . but they could detect essentially no cause-and-effect link between self-esteem and problematic behavior, whether it's teen pregnancy, drug use or child abuse (*Kirk*, A-18).

As indicting as the research is regarding self-esteem, a reading of 2 Timothy 3:1-7 will reveal what one must be most concerned about and how far many in the church, including Dobson and the Passantinos, have drifted from the truth of Scripture by promoting self-esteem.

> This know also, that in the last days perilous times shall come. For men shall be lovers of their own selves, covetous, boasters, proud, blasphemers, disobedient to parents, unthankful, unholy, without natural affection, trucebreakers, false accusers, incontinent, fierce, despisers of those that are good, traitors, heady, highminded, lovers of pleasures more than lovers of God; having a form of godliness, but denying the power thereof: from such turn away. For of this sort are they which creep into houses, and lead captive silly women laden with sins, led away with divers lusts, ever learning, and never able to come to the knowledge of the truth.

<u>The Passantinos in Concert with Collins</u>. The Passantinos say:

> Many of the techniques of psychotherapy are compatible with a Christian world view because they are not unique "psychology" discoveries or inventions but reflect the common sense, experience, and thoughtful reflection every Christian should practice as a matter of course (39).

They then refer to Collins' idea of the "intersection of psychology and the church" (39) as "overlap." This reflects the favorable influence of Gary Collins in the Passantinos' thinking. Collins believes that "Integration is not always avoidable." He says, "It would be convenient if all counseling could be divided neatly into 'the psychological way' and 'the spiritual way' with no overlapping goals, methods or assumptions" (Collins, 129). He then adds,

Even those who try to dichotomize counseling into psychological versus biblical approaches have to admit that there is overlap. Listening, talking, confessing, accepting, thinking and understanding are neither purely psychological nor exclusively biblical activities (Collins, 129).

We would disagree with him. To us anyone who bases his counseling in the Word of God is using the spiritual way; and anyone who is using the psychological opinions of men is using the psychological way. The fact that both kinds of counseling use listening, talking, and so forth is not the point The point is upon what foundation is their listening, talking, etc. based?

To use Collins' thinking, one would say that prayer by a cultist or occultist would *overlap* prayer by a Christian. Also, the fact that cultists and occultists think is in no way an open door to their theology any more than the door is left open to psychotherapy because both psychotherapists and biblicists think.

The Passantinos end this section by again quoting Collins. They say:

> Collins gives a concise statement reflective of many Christian psychologists [and the Passantinos]: "Of course there is much that is wrong about psychology—but there is also much that is sensitive, helpful, valid, and good. The best psychologists carefully sift the conclusions and evidence, reject that which is invalid and make use of the rest" (39).

We don't know how many books by Collins the Passantinos have read, possibly none, but Collins is filled with many of the same contradictory pro/con statements about psychotherapy as the Passantinos, and he also leaves the door to psychotherapy wide open for Christians. We have confronted the serious errors of Collins in Part One of our book *Prophets of PsychoHeresy I*.

Collins answers the question, "Can Secular Psychology and Christianity Be Integrated?" in the affirmative. He says,

> For the Christian psychologist, integration involves a recognition of the ultimate authority of the Bible, a willingness to learn what God has allowed humans to discover though psychology and other fields of knowledge, and a desire to determine how both scriptural truths and psychological data can enable us better to understand and help people (Collins, 127).

Collins evidently trusts more in a Christian psychologist's understanding of the Bible than a theologian's in this regard, for he says that criticisms of professional therapy "could be dismissed had they come from a journalist or a **theologian** writing as an outsider" (Collins, 17). How can a theologian be an "outsider" when psychotherapy and counseling psychologies deal with the soul of man? How can he be an "outsider" when integration involves the Bible? Collins says, "Psychological conclusions that contradict biblical principles certainly cannot be integrated with Christianity" (Collins, 128). Yet, who would know better than a biblical scholar and theologian indwelt by Christ? One does not have to be a psychologist to see the contradictions.

Collins then goes on to restate his constant theme, "It is important, therefore, that integration be done carefully, selectively, tentatively and by individuals who seek to be led by the Holy Spirit" (Collins, 128). We receive much information from individuals who have been therapized by Christian professionals, from Christian therapists who have left the profession, and from numerous others about whether or not Collins' theme is played out in practice. In addition, the Christian practitioners who participated in our survey of CAPS, described earlier, would certainly believe that they are being led by the Holy Spirit, in spite of the fact that they follow a widely divergent variety of theories and practices. There is about as much agreement among them as among their secular counterparts. In fact, some who claim to be led by the Holy Spirit use techniques from the Forum, Lifespring, and even from Eastern therapies with their emphasis on visualization and spirit guides.

Since the advent of psychotherapy, each generation has brought forth its psychotherapeutic innovators who have insisted upon the success of their systems. Dr. Jerome Frank says, "A historical overview of Western psychotherapy reveals that the dominant psychotherapeutic approach of an era reflects contemporary cultural attitudes and values" (Frank, 360). In contrast, the Bible contains eternal truths about the human condition. God has given His Word, and it serves as a healing balm for all ages. God's Word does not change with the culture or the times.

Biblical theology did without psychology for almost two thousand years. The prophets of the Old Testament, the disciples and apostles of the New Testament, and the saints right up to the present century did very well without psychology. Why would the church need the modern-day psychologizers now? We shudder to think of what a twentieth-century psychologist would have said to Ezekiel seeing "a wheel in the middle of a wheel," or to Elijah hearing "a still small voice," or Isaiah seeing "the Lord sitting upon a throne, high and lifted up," or Peter and his vision of unclean things, or the man who was caught up to the third heaven.

Gary Collins, a prime leader on the issue of integration, agreed to and then backed out of a debate which would have covered this issue. In the Preface to one of his books, Collins reminisces about "old-fashioned college debating societies" and "grand debating duels that took place in my little alma mater" (Collins, 9). He says, "I wish we could have more debaters like that today" (Collins, 10). He was reminded of this after he backed out of the debate, but still declined to meet even though the location and date had been left open to him. Since then he has become the president of the American Association of Christian Counselors, probably the largest organization of integrationists in America.

The Passantinos promise much so far, but provide little. With all their razzle-dazzle about using psychology under certain conditions, they were not able to give one example of an insight from psychotherapy and its underlying psychologies that is of any use to the Christian and they could not name one individual whose work would demonstrate what they claim. These facts alone should condemn the entire series.

4

Responding to Part Four

"The High Cost of Biblical Compassion and Commitment"

The Passantinos begin this section with a personal example of Gretchen in need of help and calling her father. The example is followed by Christians seeking help. The Passantinos say, "Christian leaders struggle to help with these problems as well, often **feeling** inadequate, untrained, and lacking the expertise to provide substantive help" (20, bold added). We contend that the reason why Christian leaders feel "inadequate and untrained" is because those in and out of the church, including the Passantinos, have intimidated them into feeling this way. At the end of the above quote, the Passantinos refer to Christian leaders "lacking the expertise to provide substantive help." The first part of the sentence was communicated as a "feeling"; the second part was expressed as a fact. This description is one reason why Christian leaders feel inadequate. We challenge the Passantinos to show research evidence that the average Christian leader is "lacking the expertise to provide substantive help." One look at the research results comparing success rates of amateurs and professionals should put a stop to this erroneous idea on their part. We encourage Christian leaders that they can more powerfully minister when they are armed with the Word of God and the power of the Spirit than psychotherapists or integrationists.

The Passantinos say:

> At first we may turn to our closest friends, or someone in our church who seems to understand. Too often, however, we don't get the help we need, and sometimes we even incur more problems from poor or inattentive counselors. Many of us suffer in silence and isolation. Many others turn to "professionals," both inside and outside the church: counselors, therapists, psychologists, and psychiatrists (20).

This is added intimidation with the door held open to psychotherapy. Compare their description of what happens when one turns to the church for help with turning to professionals for help. When one turns to the church for help, they say, "Too often, however, we don't get the help we need, and sometimes we even incur more problems from poor or inattentive counselors." The Passantinos make the church look awful in this example and yet not one criticism of individuals turning to professionals. The research actually indicates that the Passantinos' slur on the church aptly applies to professionals. Thus it should read, "Too often, however, [when we seek professional psychological counseling] we don't get the help we need, and sometimes we even incur more problems from poor or inattentive counselors." Why didn't the Passantinos reverse this? Because they are determined to keep the door open to psychotherapy.

The Passantinos on the one hand blame the church for not ministering and then turn around and represent the church in this negative manner. Is it any wonder that Christians look elsewhere? Contrary to the Passantinos, we would encourage believers that they can and should minister to one another and point out all the research evidence supporting their ability to do so. We would then recite from the extensive research that would expose the fallacies of professional psychotherapy. If amateurs who do not even know the Word of God can do as well or better than the highly trained therapists, why is it that Christians should not be able to do at least as well? The Passantinos have demonstrated throughout their series that they are unwilling to take such a position even though their articles give enough minimal information to do so.

The Passantinos make an excellent point when they say, "Human nature is complex, and much of it is only partially and imperfectly discerned through common methods of evaluation" (20). They could have used this very point to encourage the use of Scripture (God's truth) alone over the wisdom of men. But, as they do throughout the series, they ignore the deep implications of what they are saying and continue to work hard at keeping the door open to psychotherapy and its underlying psychologies.

"All Truth Is God's Truth"

One of the ways integrationists attempt to make psychotherapeutic theories and therapies acceptable to Christians is by saying, "All truth is God's truth." All kinds of speculations, imaginations, and contradictory theories and techniques have been brought in under that umbrella. The Passantinos attempt to clarify "all truth is God's truth" by saying that "since God is truth (Isa. 65:16; cf. John 14:6) and knows all things (Jer. 23:23-24), there is nothing that is actually in existence, no fact, no knowledge, and no truth—nothing that corresponds to reality—that He does not know" (21). That is an amazing explanation. Instead of explaining what is *truth* or what is *God's truth*, they are talking about what God **knows**. God knows everything, including the lies of Satan.

Discussing the statement, "All truth is God's truth," calls for a definition of *truth* and a clarification of what can be included under what is referred to as "God's truth." First of all, what is truth? While there are several definitions of truth, one generally assumes that truth represents that which is true, real, and actual. Truth is the perfect expression of that which is. If what is put into the category of "all truth" is limited to "the perfect expression of that which is," then that would be "God's truth." However, the assortment of ideas, opinions, and even seeming facts under the designation of "all truth" reduces truth to meaning "imperfect human perception of that which is."

The broad field of psychology at best involves human observation and interpretation of Creation and therefore is subject to human error and the blindness of the unregenerate heart as described in Ephesians 4:18, "Having the understanding darkened, being alienated from the life of God through the ignorance that is in them, because of the blindness of their heart."

Psychotherapy and its underlying psychologies have the further problem of subjective imagination also proceeding from unregenerate individuals. They represent a further departure from expressing that which truly is. Instead, they present some subjective observation, reasoned analysis, creative imagination, and much distortion. If these ideas are included under the declaration, "All truth is God's truth," one must conclude that those who use the expression have greatly misunderstood the nature of truth, let alone God's truth. In raising human observation, interpretation, and opinions to the same level and authority as God's truth revealed through Jesus and in the written Word of God, those who promote psychology among Christians demonstrate their high view of human opinion and their low view of Scripture.

Dr. John Carter and Dr. Bruce Narramore, both of Rosemead Graduate School of Psychology, have written a book titled *The Integration of Psychology and Theology*. Carter and Narramore refer to and repeat, "All truth is God's truth." This has obviously become the abracadabra of integrationists. The incantation is sprinkled throughout their book as it is in the writings of others who espouse the amalgamationists' position. Such books repeatedly state, but cannot support, the "all truth is God's truth" platitude. They talk about it but cannot demonstrate the connection between "all truth is God's truth" and so-called psychological truth. The lack of uniformity in psychological theories and practices among those who preach integration should prove that theological-psychological amalgamania is in a sad state of confusion.

After looking at the over 400 competing and often contradictory therapies and over 10,000 not-always-compatible techniques, and after surveying Christian therapists and finding how little consistency there is among them in what they practice and in how great the variety of their approaches, one has to conclude that the integrationists make what they call "God's truth" look more than just a little confused. When one reviews all of the research and considers all of the researchers, one can also conclude that if the integrationists are referring to psychotherapy as science, one gets the impression that God's truth must include "science falsely so-called." The use of psychotherapy in Christianity is not a testimony to science. It is a testimony to how much the church can be deceived.

In his discussion of "all truth is God's truth," John Moffat says, "I think that, in many ways, this slogan is the verbal equivalent of a graven image; something that appears to represent truth but does not" (Moffat, 27). He explains:

> None of the people that use this "all truth" expression actually say that they consider man's thoughts equal to God's revealed Word, it just happens to work that way in practice; just as at first the graven images were not meant to replace God, only to represent Him (Moffat, 28).

Then to show where "all truth is God's truth" thinking can lead a person, Moffat says:

> I can imagine Nadab and Abihu talking before the early worship service in the wilderness. One says to the other, "All fire is God's fire. God made all fire; therefore it is all of him." Or while Moses was up on Mount Sinai, the children of Israel could have said to Aaron, "All worship of God is God's worship." These analogies have the same deceptive sound of being logical at first glance, but they are full of the same ambiguity and deceit as the expression "all truth is God's truth" (Moffat, 28).

In contrast to the broad category labeled "all truth" by those who want to include what humans perceive through their senses, achieve through their reason, conceive in their minds, receive from one another, and interweave with Scripture, the specific category of "God's truth" includes only what is perfectly and flawlessly true. God Himself is true and He has made known His truth through His Son, who referred to Himself as the truth (Jn 14:6); through His written Word, which perfectly states what is true (Jn 17:17); and through the Holy Spirit, who is called the Spirit of Truth who will guide believers into all truth (Jn 16:13). With all that God has provided in His Son, His Word, and His Holy Spirit, one wonders why people are so enamored with the psychological opinions of men.

All humans have partial perception, fragmentary knowledge, and incomplete morality. While these are gifts common to all mankind, they are contaminated by human depravity. Whatever truth people have perceived is contaminated by their unrighteousness. Apart from special revelation and special grace, all unbelievers stand guilty before God, because they hold whatever truth they have gained through general revelation or common grace in a state of unrighteousness (Rom 1:18). Do such people appear to be reliable sources for Christians to seek counsel for godly living? Indeed, general revelation and common grace serve as very weak and even dangerous justifications for dipping into psychotherapy and its underlying psychologies, all of which were conceived and developed by unredeemed minds.

In contrast to their tangential explanation of "All truth is God's truth," the Passantinos actually use the statement in a manner that allows for the inclusion of psychotherapy and its underlying psychologies. Then, instead of giving an example of God's truth from psychotherapy, they mention multiplication tables.

With the "all truth is God's truth" door wide open, they say:

> However, we can come to a more complete, comprehensive understanding of human nature by a

variety of truth-gathering activities, including observation, rational evaluation, assessment, and application of what we already know to be true. Of course, every aspect of our understanding must by tested by, and conform to, the Bible, even if that aspect is not explicitly taught in Scripture (21).

The two examples they give are "multiplication tables" and "cigarette smoking." It is interesting that the Passantinos use mathematics and health science in order to prove their case for the "variety of truth-gathering activities" that they list. Using such examples reveals their faulty philosophical foundations and will lead to category errors. As we noted earlier, "A category error is an error in the use of language that, in turn, produces errors in thinking" (Leifer, 36,37). We have already mentioned earlier how this type of "observation, rational evaluation, assessment, and application of what we already know to be true" has led to gross errors when attempting to understand the complexities of human nature, particularly that which cannot be observed. But, all of the integrationists, including the Passantinos two favorites (Backus and Dobson) would deny that their use of these means has ended up in violation of Scripture. The reason the Passantinos resort to this fallacy is because they are unable to give examples from psychotherapy and its underlying psychologies. We look forward to their response in which they will stop hypothesizing and fallacying and start conceptualizing and specifying psychological theories, techniques, and therapists to prove their claim. Thus far their two prime examples (Backus and Dobson) have failed the test.

The Passantinos next quote author Dave Hunt from his book *Beyond Seduction* in reference to "All truth is God's truth":

This specious phrase is put forth whenever questions are raised and is generally accepted without further thought by those inquiring.

What is meant by *truth* is seldom elaborated. Are we talking about *scientific facts* involving the brain and body, or about God's truth involving the soul and spirit? Jesus said, "Thy Word is *truth*," not *part* of the truth. Psychotherapy deals with a subject upon which God has spoken with finality and about which He claims to have communicated in His Word the *whole truth*. There are not parts of this truth missing from the Bible and left in limbo, only to be discovered somewhere in the secular world (Hunt, *Beyond Seduction*, 137 italics in original).

To give the reader a more complete rendering of Hunt's argument, we include the above quote within it's context:

Should we not consider it odd that God has apparently inspired men such as Freud, Jung, and now more recently Maslow and Rogers with "truths" hidden to the apostles and prophets and all of the leaders in the entire history of the church until the present time? Now, we are told reassuringly, this is not to be considered strange at all. What we allegedly need to understand is: "All truth is God's truth." This specious phrase is put forth whenever questions are raised and is generally accepted without further thought by those inquiring.

What is meant by *truth* is seldom elaborated. Are we talking about *scientific facts* involving the brain and body, or about God's truth involving the soul and spirit? Jesus said, "Thy Word is *truth*," not *part* of the truth. Psychotherapy deals with a subject upon which God has spoken with finality and about which He claims to have communicated in His Word the *whole truth*. There are not parts of this truth missing from the Bible and left in limbo, only to be discovered somewhere in the secular world. To suggest that there is such a lack contradicts the clear testimony of Scripture and the consistent teaching of the church for centuries, a church that withstood the Roman arena and the Inquisition and left the stamp of victorious Christian living and the blood of her martyrs upon the pages of history long before Freud or his successors came upon the scene.

It is one thing to say that it was inspiration from God, at least in a general sense, that led to the discovery of polio vaccine or atomic theory. It is quite another matter to say that God inspired Freud with insight into methods of diagnosing and treating the soul and spirit of man. And it is equally dangerous to suggest that anti-Christians have been inspired to fill a missing portion of the truth that God Himself declares He has already revealed in its fullness in His Holy Word. The very idea of a *Christian* psychology violates basic biblical principles, and increasing numbers of those once involved are beginning to see this and to reject this false religion. Typical of many responses received to *The Seduction of Christianity* is the following excerpt from a letter:

> I am delighted that there is something coming on the [book-store] shelves telling the truth.
> I majored in psychology, but am ashamed of it. After becoming a Christian, I realized that psychology is a false religion, but sure have a hard time convincing anyone of that fact.

Paul wrote, ". . . the things of God knoweth no man but by the Spirit of God." It is clear in the context that he is not talking about scientific discoveries made by atheists through an insight into nature or the witness of moral conscience that God gives to all men. Paul is referring not to *natural* but to *spiritual* truths, which he specifically states are revealed by God only to true believers (Hunt, *Beyond Seduction*, 137-138).

Hunt also declares:

The Christian life is not a grit-your-teeth and hold-your-breath roller-coaster ride. It is Christ living His resurrection life in those who have opened their hearts to Him. To suggest that psychotherapeutic techniques lately discovered by Freud et al. are now necessary in order for today's Christian to experience the abundant life in Christ is destructive of the very faith that the proponents of this teaching say they are trying to enhance (Hunt, *Beyond Seduction*, 139).

After quoting Hunt, the Passantinos say,

We agree that the Bible contains all of the basic principles for personal development and problem resolution, and certainly the entirety of what is necessary for reconciliation with God through Christ's death on the cross, which results in our ultimate personal fulfillment in heavenly glory (Rom. 8:28-30).

Then, as if in contrast to what Hunt said, they say, "We do *not* agree that the Bible contains all of the details and/or applications of all of the basic principles for human problem resolution" (22). Hunt would agree with their first statement, but this second statement turns out to be a straw man fallacy. Unfortunately there are many instances of logical fallacies used throughout this series. The Passantinos have grossly misrepresented Dave Hunt's position. To prove our point, we ask that the Passantinos provide us with the name of one individual who has ever said, agreed with, or supported the idea that "the Bible contains **all** of the details and/or applications of **all** of the basic principles for human problem resolution." One would have to be stupid to make such a statement and one would have to be desperate to use it as an accusation.

The Passantinos then say, "Hunt and some other BCM advocates take 1 Peter 1:3 out of context and apply it to all areas of human fulfillment" (22). Of course they are really referring to 2 Peter 1:3, when they say:

> The verse reads, "His divine power has given us everything we need for life and godliness through our knowledge of him who called us by his own glory and goodness." Its context is *salvation*, not the details of daily human living (22, italics in original).

However, 2 Peter 1:3, read in context and in checking with the original Greek, leads one to conclude that this verse includes the entirety of salvation, which includes justification, sanctification, and glorification. Salvation in its entirety does include the details of daily human living. All commentaries we checked supported this understanding. Numerous verses support this view of salvation, including Philippians 2:12-13, addressed to believers: "Wherefore, my beloved, as ye have always obeyed, not as in my presence only, but now much more in my absence, work out your own salvation with fear and trembling. For it is God which worketh in you both to will and to do of his good pleasure." Does this not have to do with daily living? The Passantinos reveal a very limited view of salvation.

We think the Passantinos' quoting and then criticizing Hunt probably has more to do with their antipathy towards Hunt than the reality of what he said. We print Hunt's reply as follows:

> While warning that Christianized psychology isn't perfect, the Passantinos promote it and deny the *sufficiency* of the Bible. (Similar confusion is expressed in the December 1995 *New Covenant,* a leading Catholic charismatic magazine.) In their final article the Passantinos state,
>
>> The Biblical Counseling Movement (BCM) ... falls short of a comprehensive program [quite an indictment of the Bible!] . . . . [Dave] Hunt and some other BCM advocates take I (sic) Peter 1:3 out of context . . . . The verse reads, "His divine power has given us everything we need for life and godliness. . . ." Its context is *salvation,* not the details of daily human living. [Dave is not part of the BCM movement.]
>
> On the contrary, one could hardly say that "life" means only *eternal life* in heaven; and surely "godliness" involves our behavior here on earth. The *context* continues: "Whereby are given unto us exceeding great and precious promises: that by these ye might be partakers of the divine nature...." Peter then exhorts to diligence, virtue, knowledge, temperance, patience, godliness and brotherly kindness, which are to characterize the very "daily human living" which the Passantinos claim is not Peter's subject.

Does the "divine nature" within us need psychological help? No! Peter assures us that "if ye do these things ye shall never fall. . ." (v 10). Paul agrees that through heeding biblical "doctrine . . . reproof . . . correction. . . [and] instruction in righteousness . . . the man [or woman] of God may be perfect, throughly furnished unto every good work" (2 Tm 3:1617). The Bible is *sufficient.* Even the watered-down NAS says, "adequate, equipped for every good work."

The Passantinos assure us that the Bible, lacking the new wisdom of Freud, et al., is deficient in its understanding of "human nature" and therefore needs to be supplemented with psychology. They offer Christian psychology's new good news for the troubled heart: humanist apostles of psychology have discovered new truths to make up for biblical deficiency and to provide the church at last with the understanding and tools it has lacked for 1,900 years. They write,

> [N]ot everything about human nature is completely explained in Scripture . . . we can come to a more complete, comprehensive understanding of human nature by a variety of [lately discovered] truth-gathering activities, including observation, rational evaluation, assessment, and application of what we already know to be true....

The CRI articles reflect a tragic misunderstanding of what Jesus meant by "truth" when He said, "If ye continue in my word, then are ye my disciples indeed; and ye shall know the truth, and the truth shall make you free" (Jn 8:3132). The Passantinos consider anything factual to be part of "God's truth":

"100 times 100 equals 10,000, and we can count on that as 'God's truth' because it corresponds to reality...." On the contrary, the Jews would have readily acknowledged that 100 times 100 equals 10,000— yet Christ said they would not believe *the truth.*

Jesus promised that through obedience to His Word His disciples would know the truth, *all* of it, not *part* of it. It takes just three verses to expose the folly of the Passantinos' (and Christian psychology's) position: "Even the Spirit of truth; whom the world cannot receive..." (Jn 14: 17); "[T]he Spirit of truth. .. will guide you into all truth" (16:13); "But the natural man receiveth not the things of the Spirit of God: for they are foolishness unto him: neither can he know them, because they are spiritually discerned" (1 Cor 2:14).

If the Spirit of truth guides into *all truth,* and the world cannot receive or know Him, nor can the natural man receive His truth, then the world knows not *the truth.* When Jesus said to Pilate, "I came to bear witness unto *the truth"* (Jn 18:37), He didn't mean science, much less psychology. Nor did He mean worldly wisdom when He said, "[B]ecause I tell you *the truth,* ye believe me not" (8:45). Clearly, the article reflects a false view of what Christ meant by *the truth.* Only the Holy Spirit teaches *the truth,* and only to those whom He indwells and guides. This truth alone can set men free from fear, anxiety, insecurity, selfishness, anger, frustration, a sense of hopelessness and inadequacy and the other symptoms of sin.

Paul writes, "Now we have received, not the spirit of the world, but the spirit which is of God; that we might know the things that are freely given to us of God" (1 Cor 2:12). The "things that are freely given to us of God" are sufficient for "life and godliness" and to make us "Perfect, throughly furnished unto every good work." Paul continues: "Which things also we speak, not in the words which man's wisdom teacheth, but which the Holy Ghost teacheth. . . .

In contrast to Paul, the Passantinos consider at least some of "the words which man's wisdom teacheth" to be an essential supplement to *the truth* of God's Word. God promises, however, that "love, joy, peace, longsuffering, gentleness, goodness, faith, meekness, temperance" are the "fruit of the *Spirit*' (Gal 5:22-23), *not* the fruit of *therapy*. (Hunt, "Would you please respond," italics in original).

The Passantinos say, "Using Scripture as our foundation, we can learn additionally from observation, experimentation, the experiences of others, and rational evaluation" (22). As we have already demonstrated in our critique of Part Three, this repetitious message of theirs is a pipe dream. It is both biblically errant and practically unrealizable. It is biblically errant to think that puny man will learn about the depths of mankind by the means claimed by them. Visible superficialities—yes; the meaningful depths—no!

Proof that it is practically unrealizable is the fact that there are numerous Christian psychotherapists who claim to be using "Scripture as a foundation" who use conflicting and contradictory systems and techniques from one another. Which ones "learned" from the means listed? The Passantinos themselves provided two "excellent" examples (Backus and Dobson) who, with all their care, caution and concern, have failed to learn from the means the Passantinos list, "Using Scripture as our foundation."

The Passantinos declare:

For the careful Christian thinker, "all truth is God's truth" reflects the appreciation of the complexity of God's plan, His implementation of His will through a variety of means, and the overarching supremacy of the Bible as the perfect repository of His eternal standards (22).

The not too subtle repetitious communication is that if we are a "careful Christian thinker," we will leave the door open to psychotherapy as they did.

Continuing this impossible dream, the Passantinos say:

Before society became dichotomized between the church and the world, Christians used the Bible as the embodiment of God's standard, and assumed that learning in science, philosophy, the arts, and mathematics applied God's standard to all aspects of life. Christians did not choose *between* the Bible and science—science *complemented* Scripture and *was founded on Scripture* (22, italics in original).

What exactly do the Passantinos mean when they say, "Before society became dichotomized between the church and the world"? The night He was betrayed, Jesus prayed,

And now I am no more in the world, but these are in the world, and I come to thee. Holy Father, keep through thine own name those whom thou hast given me, that they may be one, as we are. While I was with them in the world, I kept them in thy name: those that thou gavest me I have kept, and none of them is lost, but the son of perdition; that the scripture might be fulfilled. And now come I to thee; and these things I speak in the world, that they might have my joy fulfilled in themselves. I have given them thy word; and the world hath hated them, because they are not of the world, even as I am not of the world. I pray not that thou shouldest take them out of the world, but that thou shouldest keep them from the evil. They are not of the world, even as I am not of the world. Sanctify them through thy truth: thy word is truth. As thou hast sent me into the world, even so have I also sent them into the world (Jn 17:11-18).

Christ and the Apostles made a clear distinction between the church and the world. However, the Passantinos sound as if this distinction is something that happened and never should have, as if what is out there in "science, philosophy, the arts, and mathematics" is neutral. What they fail to realize is that this argument does not allow for the intrusion of psychotherapy and its underlying psychologies into the church, because these are not simply the world of "science, philosophy, the arts, and mathematics." The world's way of viewing humanity through psychotherapy and its underlying psychologies is an intrusion because God has already spoken in this area. We are not talking about the world of observation. We are talking about the intrusion into the realm of the soul, because that is what psychotherapy aims at, the inner person, the thinking, the motivation, the heart, which only God can know, evaluate, change, heal, restore, and replace. The world of "science, philosophy, the arts, and mathematics" is not the same as the nonphysical realm of the human. Then when the Passantinos speak of the Bible and science they have moved out of the realm of psychotherapy and its underlying psychologies, because those are not science, but rather "science falsely so-called" (1 Tim. 6:20), which Paul warns Timothy to avoid.

The Passantinos speak of "a false isolation," a "traditional biblical view toward living," and repeat their shibboleth:

> . . . we will be able to use those aspects of psychology that are in harmony with Scripture. Areas from which we can benefit include the observation of human behavior, educational techniques, rational evaluation, practical wisdom , and practical experience. Each of these areas, we stress, must be understood and applied according to a biblical world view, not in isolation from or in opposition to a biblical world view (22).

One repetitive line of the Passantinos' reasoning rests upon whether or not this type of psychology is science. The issue is psychotherapy and the church, not science and the church, not philosophy and the church, not the arts and the church, or even mathematics and the church. Nowhere have the Passantinos shown the connection between psychotherapy and science, but their continued switching of subjects sustains their psychotheology. The repetition of this science-psychology relationship will not establish the fallacious as factual.

The Passantinos give an example of anxiety to supposedly prove what they have been saying. Their approach is contingent upon someone discovering different approaches to help the anxious person. They contend that "we will be able to use those aspects of psychology that are in harmony with Scripture" (22). They even declare, "Many of the 'truths' that can be brought to bear on personal problems within a biblical context are discoverable even if the discoverer does not personally hold a biblical world view" (23). Having studied psychology and psychotherapeutic systems for many years, we can testify to the fact that there are many systems, developed by many who do not "hold a biblical world view," many of which are contradictory to one another. Yet these systems are used by various Christian psychotherapists who will tell you that they are not in violation of Scripture. And, the big question is: Where does sinful living and unconfessed sin come into the equation of dealing with anxiety? Anxiety reduction often becomes the **goal** of the Passantinos and integrationists rather than the *result* of dealing with it in a godly way.

We recommend an opposite-to-the-Passantinos approach. Learn the Scriptures and learn them well; live the Life and walk the Walk; as a believer uses the Bible with someone who is anxious, God will give wisdom as to what to do. This is the biblical way. After all, it was less than 50 years ago that psychologists were first licensed. What the Passantinos recommend is, to put it mildly, a mishmash of the wisdom of men and the wisdom of God, which ends up transmogrifying the truth of God.

Psalm 111:10 states, "The fear of the Lord is the beginning of wisdom." James 1:5 reveals, "If any of you lack wisdom, let him ask of God, that giveth to all men liberally, and upbraideth not; and it shall be given him." In 1 Corinthians 2:9, Paul exhorts believers: "That your faith should not stand in the wisdom of men, but in the power of God." Christians who fear the Lord will seek God when they lack wisdom. By so doing they draw out of Scripture. The Passantinos, Coe, and the Christian psychotherapists continually read into Scripture what they mean to check out with Scripture. They take the wisdom of men with the intent of checking it out with Scripture, but end up reading it into Scripture. Isn't this why there is such a multitude of contradictory psychotherapeutic systems being used by Christians? And, all in harmony with Scripture, they claim. The Passantinos and psychologists they quote take James 1:5 and seem to make it read, "If any of you lack wisdom, let him ask of the wisdom of men, that is available to all men liberally, and upbraideth not; and it shall be given him to find it in Scripture."

If this system of amalgamating the wisdom of men and the Word of God is so effective, the Passantinos should be able to demonstrate that what they recommend works biblically in practice. Let them produce the evidence that their hypothetical ideas lead to one iota better results than what the church had been doing prior to the era of the psychologized church. The burden of proof is on them.

The balance of this section of the Passantinos involves repeating the same fallacious reasoning presented up to this point regarding how "Christian therapists must keep their biblical theology at the core of their practice." They support their position by quoting three integrationists who would support the Passantinos' failed formula and who have failed at the formula themselves.

"The Cost of Congregational Commitment"

The Passantinos say, "The popularity of psychology in the church today is directly attributable to the failure of Christians to assume their proper responsibilities" (23). They also say, "However . . . the professional therapist is filling a gap that should be filled by a congregation of people who are committed mutually to each other" (42). In the Passantinos Part One section on "Biblical Counseling" they blame the church for believers seeking psychotherapy. In this section they blame believers. As we have said earlier, the Passantinos do not recognize that they are part of the reason why believers look elsewhere. The Passantinos blame the church, they blame the believer, and they leave the door open to psychotherapy, which reinforces the false message being promoted by integrationists such as Larry Crabb and others they quote.

Much of this section is devoted to Larry Crabb. Crabb has been one of the leading integrationists of psychology and Christianity. His brand of integration is not only for counseling those who are suffering problems of living, but also for all Christians to help them mature in their walk with the Lord. However, his teachings and techniques are heavily dependent on psychological theories devised by Sigmund Freud, Alfred Adler, Albert Ellis, Abraham Maslow, and others.

Crabb wrote *Basic Principles of Biblical Counseling* in 1975 and *Effective Biblical Counseling* in 1977. From the very beginning he argued that Christians could and should glean from secular psychological theories. To illustrate how secularists might have something to offer Christianity, Crabb wrote:

> Man is responsible (Glasser) to believe truth which will result in responsible behavior (Ellis) that will provide him with meaning, hope (Frankl), and love (Fromm) and will serve as a guide (Adler) to effective living with others as a self- and other-accepting person (Harris), who understands himself (Freud), who appropriately expresses himself (Perls), and who knows how to control himself (Skinner) (Crabb, *Effective Biblical Counseling*, 56, parentheses in original).

During the 80s Crabb added more titles. When we would describe Crabb's theories, people would say, "But, have you read his latest book?" as if he had changed. However, each time we found that, though his language had changed to sound more evangelical and less psychological, certain psychological concepts remained in place. They were simply described differently.

Central to Crabb's model of man are two dominant unconscious needs that motivate behavior. In his earlier books Crabb called the two unconscious needs "security" and "significance." Later he changed his terminology to "longings" for "relationship and impact." Crabb clearly indicates that his change in words does not involve any change in the doctrine. In *Understanding People*, he says:

> Readers familiar with my earlier books will recognize movement in my concepts but not, I think, fundamental change. For example, my preference now is to speak of *deep longings in the human heart for relationship and impac*t rather than *personal needs for security and significance* (Crabb, 15, italics in original).

In our book *Prophets of PsychoHeresy I*, we show that Crabb's doctrine of a powerful unconscious is based on the Freudian unconscious as modified by Alfred Adler. Crabb says in *Understanding People*:

> Freud is rightly credited with introducing the whole idea of *psychodynamics* to the modern mind. The term refers to psychological forces within the personality (usually unconscious) that have the power to cause behavioral and emotional disturbance. He taught us to regard problems as *symptoms* of underlying *dynamic processes* in the psyche (Crabb, 59, italics in original).

Crabb further says, "I think Freud was correct. . . when he told us to look beneath surface problems to hidden internal causes" (Crabb, *Understanding People:*, 61). While Crabb does not agree with all that Freud taught and even sees errors in his theories, he contends that "the error of Freud and other dynamic theorists is *not* an insistence that we pay close attention to unconscious forces within personality" (Crabb, *UP*, 61, italics his). In spite of Freud's strong criticism of Christianity, Crabb says, "I believe that [Freud's] psychodynamic theory is both provocative and valuable in recognizing elements in the human personality that many theologians have failed to see" (Crabb, *UP*, 215-216).

In his earlier books Crabb uses the word *unconscious* directly and explains its hidden nature and power for motivation. In *Inside Out* he relies on metaphors and descriptive phrases such as "heart," "core," "beneath the surface," "hidden inner regions of our soul," "dark regions of our soul," "beneath the waterline," "underlying motivation," "hidden purpose," and "reservoir of their self-protective energy." The very title *Inside Out* suggests the Freudian notion of the unconscious. Crabb clearly presents the unconscious as a real and powerful part of every person. He also suggests that doctrines of the unconscious are indispensable to the church!

A dominant characteristic of Crabb's integration for both counseling and sanctification for believers is a necessity of feeling the pain of the past before one can change one's "current relational style." Crabb says:

> The first act of changing his current relational style had to be to open himself to feeling the pain of his past. Only then would he be in a position to realize how deeply determined he was to never feel that pain again. . . moving on to deeper levels of involvement with others required this man to more deeply feel his pain and to face his self-protective sin. The more deeply we enter our disappointment, the more thoroughly we can face our sin. **Unless we feel the pain of being victimized**, we will tend to limit the definition of our problem with sin to visible acts of transgression (Crabb, *Inside Out*, 186, bold added).

"*The High Cost of Biblical Compassion & Commitment*" 133

In his *Inside Out* Film Series, Crabb taught that exposing the unconscious needs, fears, pains, and wrong strategies is a necessary means for personal Christian growth (sanctification). He said this is the way people become truly dependent on God:

> Until we admit that nothing and no one else really satisfies, we're never going to depend on Christ. And the **only way** to admit that there is no real satisfaction apart from Christ is to feel the disappointment in every other relationship (Film 2).

Because of a *Christianity Today* interview of Crabb with the words "Larry Crabb's Antipsychology Crusade" on the cover of the August 14, 1995 issue, people were again thinking that Crabb might be turning around. But what he is actually doing is trying to bring his psychological ideas into the church for elders to use in ministry. In his 1995 talk at Moody he confessed:

> As an active member of the Christian Counseling Movement for the past 25 years, I'm beginning to wonder if in the middle of the considerable good that I think we have done—and I'm not anti-counseling, **I'm not anti-professional counseling at all**, I think a lot of good has been done by Godly Christian counselors, don't misunderstand me— but I wonder if in the middle of the considerable good that Godly Christian counselors who operate in the professional setting have done, if perhaps without knowing it, certainly without intending it, if we have unwittingly helped to weave into the fabric of evangelical Christianity a very bad idea—an idea that has strengthened our dependence on counseling experts while weakening our confidence in what Godly

elders could do if encouraged and released to honor their calling (bold added).

While Crabb may be beginning to realize some of the things some of us have been teaching for years, he has not repudiated his past and continues to inject psychology into his teachings. And from what Crabb said at the Moody conference, it sounds as if he will continue the same processing of reliving painful disappointments in the past.

In spite of the *Christianity Today* headlines, it is obvious that Crabb still supports his past books, his psychologized model of "biblical counseling," counseling for pay, and the ungodly and unbiblical American Association of Christian Counselors. Crabb made it ultimately clear in a follow-up letter to the editor of *Christianity Today* that he is not anti-psychology. He wrote:

> I am neither crusading against psychology nor do I want to put an end to Christian psychology. . . . Positioning me as an antipsychology crusader who wants to end Christian psychology is badly inaccurate and places me in company where I don't belong. I am a friend of Christian counseling; **I am not part of the antipsychology movement**; and I am grateful for the many godly men and women who faithfully represent Christ in their professional counseling (October 2, 1995, bold added).

The Passantinos rightly admit that Crabb is an integrationist but wrongly promote his open door to psychotherapy. They end this section by quoting Crabb. They say:

> Larry Crabb notes that "since we're never going to get [the ideal functioning church], there will always

be a place [for professional counselors]. There's obviously a need for professional counselors for hurting folks who cannot find the kind of help that should be available elsewhere (42, brackets by the Passantinos).

When the Passantinos, Crabb, and other integrationists send ambivalent messages to believers it's no wonder they end up in the offices of psychotherapists.

"How To Find a Good Counselor"

The Passantinos give "Specific questions for a prospective counselor" (43). However the answer from the research for some of the questions is simply: It doesn't matter; so why ask? The psychotherapists' answers to the following questions the Passantinos recommend asking really do not matter:

"What branch or school of psychology (analytic/dynamic, behavioral, or humanistic) represents your (the counselor's) educational background?"

"What is your highest earned educational degree related to your counseling work?"

"How long have you been a professional counselor?"

The Passantinos' questions reveal their inadequate understanding of the research and serve to further leave the door wide open to the psychotherapist's office. As we said in Part One,

. . . because of their ignorance, they fail to quote the research that demonstrates that "the training, credentials, and experience of psychotherapists are irrelevant" (Dawes, 62). The common elements in therapy, used by both amateurs and professionals, that contribute to change are common in many kinds of interpersonal relationships and not dependent upon training, credentials, or experience.

Instead of the Passantinos' pro-psychology jargon about "How To Find a Good Counselor," we would quote the following from Dr. Robyn Dawes, professor a Carnegie-Mellon University and a widely-recognized researcher on psychological evaluations:

> Virtually all the research—and this book will reference more than three hundred empirical investigations and summaries of investigations—has found that these professionals' claims to superior intuitive insight, understanding, and skill as therapists are simply invalid. What our society has done, sadly, is to license such people to "do their own thing," while simultaneously justifying that license on the basis of scientific knowledge, which those licensed too often ignore. This would not be too bad if "their own thing" had some validity, but it doesn't. What the license often does is to provide a governmental sanction for nonsense (Dawes, 8).

One additional question the Passantinos ask is, "What insurance do you accept?" Such a question implies that the Passantinos are open to insurance coverage for counseling. However, all the insurance companies we have interviewed have told us that insurance coverage requires that the "mental health professional must function within the scope of his license," i.e. if he is a licensed psychologist, he must give psychological services. No company we interviewed permitted coverage for biblical counseling. All the companies required a mental health code designation for services. Probably the Passantinos do not know enough about this area to issue a warning.

In this final section, the Passantinos continue to leave the door open to psychology. They repeat their rhetoric, rationalization and reason for writing this series by stating, "It is always preferable to find a counselor who has adequate training in both biblical theology and sound principles of counseling from the Bible and from other sources (always tested by the Bible)" (42). We are in radical disagreement with the Passantinos. It is preferable to find a counselor who does **not** have "adequate training . . . in principles of counseling. . . from other sources," but rather a fellow believer who knows Scripture and has lived it for years. In other words, just find a mature believer who would rather trust only in God's wisdom and will not attempt to dilute it with the psychological wisdom of men. As to their parenthesized caution, "always tested by the Bible," we have already said the Passantinos will not find one Christian psychotherapist who will say that his/her psychology is contrary to the Bible.

To complete this article and the series, the Passantinos give "Specific Considerations" for "How to Find a Good Counselor." In this last section there is a dramatic contrast between the Passantinos leaving the door open to psychotherapy and a testimony by Gretchen Passantino that should have been the exclamation mark to closing the door to psychotherapy.

Gretchen Passantino tells about a personal situation at the beginning of this fourth part and then says:

> I was depressed, tired, distressed over our sick children, in a panic over our finances, and dangerously close to accusing God of neglecting us. I needed a good counselor, and I knew of no counselor better than my dad (20).

In this last section she describes how her own father's dying counsel was of great help to her. No death and dying therapy for her father and no grief therapist for her and her family were mentioned in the account.

While the Passantinos missed a number of the complexities of psychotherapy and its underlying psychologies, they did learn enough in their brief excursion through the subject to reject all of it. The poignant and dramatic story about Gretchen's father should have been the coup de grace against psychotherapy and its underlying psychologies in the church. But, all it did was to demonstrate the extent to which the Passantinos and other integrationists are willing to go to maintain the popular belief in the wisdom of men. One could take the various parts of what the Passantinos have said in their four-part series and have a strong case against psychotherapy and for the Bible, but that is not what they do. The bottom line is that the Passantinos and CRI have come down clearly on the side of supporting the open door to psychotherapy and its underlying psychologies. The integrationists and practitioners are cheering loudly about this CRI open door approach. The Lord said through Isaiah, "Woe to the rebellious children, saith the LORD, that take counsel, but not of me; and that cover with a covering, but not of my spirit, that they may add sin to sin" (Is 30:1).

In the book of Nehemiah, Tobiah opposed and ridiculed the building of the wall. When the temple was restored, Tobiah was given a room in the house of the Lord. But, when Nehemiah heard about it he threw Tobiah out (Neh 4:3; 6:1; 13:4-9; 1 Ki 11:2,3). This is what needs to be done with the Tobiah of psychotherapy in the church. Psychotherapy, with its false promises and facade of science, needs to be purged from the church so that Christians will once more bear "one another's burdens, and so fulfil the law of Christ" (Gal 6:2).

In response to the fourth part of the Passantino series, a letter to the editor was printed in the *Christian Research Journal*. With permission of the author, we reproduce the letter as follows:

> I was saddened when I read "Psychology and the Church (Part Four): The High Cost of Biblical Compassion and Commitment" in your Fall 1995 issue. Human reason seems reasonable until it is brought to the light of Scripture. History states that psychology is rooted in philosophy, not science.
>
> A significant statement is made by Paul in Romans 11:16: "If the root is holy, so are the branches." The opposite is also true: If the root is unholy, so are the branches. Examine the five greatest roots of psychology, and you will find atheists (Freud, Skinner, and Erickson) and men who outright denied Christ (Rogers and Jung). I look at the root of psychology and see Christianity intertwining itself in the branches of modern psychotherapy and wonder what it is doing in *Christian Research Journal*.
>
> The tares have been sown. They are growing up with the wheat. Everywhere, in almost every church, pastors have been trained in psychology and/or have psychologically trained counselors available. I do not believe psychology will stand the fire of the judgment seat of Christ because it is of man, not of God. In the meantime, however, as the tares and the wheat grow together, I was saddened when I saw an article affirming the tares in a fine magazine like *Christian Research Journal*.

CRI should have listened to this writer instead of the Passantinos. This brief response exhibited far more discernment than Hanegraaff and the Passantinos.

A pastor wrote to CRI regarding the Passantino articles. His letter was not published or even answered. We quote from his letter as follows:

> I am deeply disappointed with CRI for publishing the biblically anemic articles by the Passantinos. . . . For a ministry that seeks to uphold God's truth, CRI needs to do some radical self-evaluation. The bottom line, which the Passantinos dodge, is: Is the Bible true in all it affirms or not? If it is, does it affirm that it is adequate to equip us for every good work (2 Tim 3:16-17)? Does it claim to provide us with all we need for life and godliness (a fairly comprehensive claim, it would seem, 2 Pet 1:3-4)?
>
> . . .
>
> Certainly, CRI readers deserve better than this unbiblical attempt to keep the flood-gates open for worldly wisdom to continue polluting God's people.... Perhaps we need a ministry to watch the cult-watching ministries like CRI if they can't even blow the whistle on such blatant psychobabble that is turning confused Christians away from the only fountain of living waters (Jer 2:13).

It is sad that the Passantinos and CRI are not willing to pay "The High Cost of . . . Commitment" to the truth of God over the psychological wisdom of men. The CRI/Passantino trust in psychological wisdom and their commitment to psychotherapy and its underlying psychologies, under any conditions, are indeed psychoheresy. The support of psychotherapy and its underlying psychologies under whatever conditions is an opprobrium in the church, but few of God's people realize it.

Postscript One

Our response to the CRI/Passantino series may seem a bit belated, coming a little over two years after the series was printed. However, between the time the Passantino series was published and now, we were involved in other ministry projects, including writing two books, *Competent to Minister: The Biblical Care of Souls* and *The End of "Christian Psychology."* Our book titled *The End of "Christian Psychology"* may be of interest to those who want more evidence for what we say in this critique. *The End of "Christian Psychology"* includes enough research evidence and information to shut down the "Christian Psychology" Industry. Unlike the Passantinos' brief research efforts, we have been researching and writing in this area for over thirty years. *The End of "Christian Psychology"* is a compendium of the latest research in the area of psychotherapy and its underlying psychologies.

The Passantinos will claim that they researched the area well but there are gaping holes in their knowledge. For example, after completing their research and even after writing the articles neither one of them had ever heard of the Stephen Ministries. This ministry is a highly visible, internationally-known program. Stephen Ministries refer to what they do as a one-to-one caring ministry. Information from Stephen Ministries reports involvement with "6,000 congregations and organizations in 17 countries, representing 78 denominations," and training over "25,000 church leaders" (letter on file) When asked about this on a radio interview, the Passantinos revealed that they had not even heard about Stephen Ministries. The interviewer had to clue them in. The Stephen Ministries is an excellent example of what the Passantinos promote in this series, because the organization trains people to minister care to one another, and it is also a referral system out through the open door to professional psychotherapy.

Postscript Two

Our primary objection to the use of psychotherapy and Christian psychology is not based merely on its confused state of self-contradiction or its phony scientific facade. Our primary objection is not even based on the attempts to explain human behavior through personal opinion presented as scientific theory. **Our greatest objection to psychotherapy and Christian psychology is that, without proof or justification, it has compromised the Word of God, the power of the cross, and the work of the Holy Spirit among Christians.**

How long shall Christians halt between psychological opinions and biblical truth? Christians have a living God, the source of all life and healing. They have His living Word. His Word contains the balm of Gilead for the troubled soul. His Word ministers grace and restoration to the mind, the will, and the emotions. We pray that the Lord will fully restore the cure of souls ministry to the church. We pray that He will use pastors, elders, and other members of the Body of Christ who will confidently stand on the completeness of God's Word and minister under the anointing of God's Holy Spirit. We pray that all Christians will rely on God's principles outlined in His Word, serve as a priesthood of all believers, and minister God's love, grace, mercy, faithfulness, wisdom, and truth to those who are suffering from problems of living. We pray that many will voluntarily give their time to love, pray, and serve to lift the heavy burdens. We pray that believers will fulfill Paul's admonition:

> Brethren, if a man be overtaken in a fault, ye which are spiritual, restore such an one in the spirit of meekness; considering thyself, lest thou also be tempted. Bear one another's burdens, and so fulfill the law of Christ (Galatians 6:1-2).

The Lord has indeed promised more to His church than a Dead Sea. He has promised living water!

> In the last day, that great day of the feast, Jesus stood and cried, saying, If any man thirst, let him come unto me, and drink. He that believeth on me, as the scripture hath said, out of his belly shall flow rivers of living water (John 7:37-38).

Is not the Lord, the Creator of the universe, able to fulfill His promises? He has promised life and life abundant! Surely we can believe Him! His faithfulness is unto all generations!

> Ho, every one that thirsteth, come ye to the waters, and he that hath no money; come ye, buy and eat; yea, come, buy wine and milk without money and without price.
>
> Wherefore do ye spend money for that which is not bread? and your labour for that which satisfieth not? hearken diligently unto me, and eat ye that which is good, and let your soul delight itself in fatness.
>
> Incline your ear, and come unto me: hear, and your soul shall live. . . .
>
> For my thoughts are not your thoughts, neither are your ways my ways, saith the Lord.

For as the heavens are higher than the earth, so are my ways higher than your ways, and my thoughts than your thoughts (Isaiah 55:1-3, 8, 9).

Ho, every one that thirsteth, come ye to the waters. . . .

References

Adler, Jonathan. "Open Minds and the Argument from Ignorance." *Skeptical Inquirer* (Jan/Feb 1998), 41-44.

Andersen, Hans Christian. *The Emperor's New Clothes*. New York: Golden Press.

Astin, Alexander W. "The Functional Autonomy of Psychotherapy" in *The Investigation of Psychotherapy: Commentaries and Readings*. Arnold P. Goldstein and Sanford J. Dean, eds. New York: John Wiley, 1966.

Backus, William and Marie Chapian. *Telling Yourself the Truth*. Minneapolis: Bethany House Publishers, 1980.

Bergin, Allen and Sol Garfield, eds. *Handbook of Psychotherapy and Behavior Change*, 4th Ed. New York: John Wiley & Sons, Inc., 1994.

Bobgan, Martin and Deidre. *Prophets of PsychoHeresy I*. Santa Barbara, CA: EastGate Publishers, 1989.

Bobgan, Martin and Deidre. *Prophets of PsychoHeresy II*. Santa Barbara, CA: EastGate Publishers, 1990.

Bobgan, Martin and Deidre. *The End of "Christian Psychology."* Santa Barbara, CA: EastGate Publishers, 1997.

Bookman, Doug. "General Revelation." Position Paper, The Master's College, Newhall, CA.

Bookman, Doug. "In Defense of Biblical Counseling." Position Paper, The Master's College, Newhall, CA.

Carter, John and Bruce Narramore. *The Integration of Psychology and Theology*. Grand Rapids: Zondervan Publishing House, 1979.

Collins Gary R. *Can You Trust Psychology?* Downers Grove: InterVarsity Press, 1988.

Crabb, Lawrence J., Jr. *Effective Biblical Counseling.* Grand Rapids: Zondervan Publishing House, 1975.

Crabb, Lawrence J., Jr. *Inside Out.* Colorado Springs: NavPress, 1988.

Crabb, Lawrence J., Jr. *Understanding People.* Grand Rapids: Zondervan Publishing House, 1987.

Craigen, Trevor. *An Exegetical Foundation for a Biblical Approach to Thinking of Oneself.* Doctoral Dissertation for Grace Theological Seminary, Winona Lake, IN, 1984.

Dawes, Robyn M. *House of Cards: Psychology and Psychotherapy Built on Myth.* New York: Free Press/Macmillan, Inc., 1994.

Dewart, Debbie. "Psychology—Friend or Fraud?" Newport Beach, CA: Discernment Publications.

Dobson, James. *Dare to Discipline.* Wheaton, IL: Tyndale House Publishers, Inc., 1970.

Dobson, James. *Hide or Seek*, Revised Edition. Old Tappan, NJ: Fleming H. Revell Company, 1979.

Dobson, James. "Little Ones Belong to Him." *TableTalk* (December 1988).

Dobson, James. *What Wives Wish Their Husbands Knew about Women.* Wheaton, IL: Tyndale House Publishers, Inc., 1975.

Ellis, Albert. "The Case Against Religion: A Psychotherapist's View" and "The Case Against Religiosity." New York: The Institute for Rational Emotive Behavior Therapy.

Ellis, Albert. *Humanistic Psychotherapy: The Rational-Emotive Approach.* New York: The Julian Press, Inc., 1973.

Ellis, Albert. *Reason and Emotion.* New York: Lyle Stuart, 1962.

References

Epstein, Robert. "Why Shrinks Have So Many Problems." *Psychology Today* (July/Aug 1997).

Frank, Jerome, "Therapeutic Factors in Psychotherapy." *American Journal of Psychotherapy*, 25 (1971).

Freedheim, Donald K., ed. *History of Psychotherapy: A Century of Change.* Washington, DC: American Psychological Association, 1992.

Fuller, Robert. *Mesmerism and the American Cure of Souls.* Philadelphia: University of Pennsylvania Press, 1982.

Goleman, Daniel. "An Eastern Toe in the Stream of Consciousness," *Psychology Today* (January 1981).

Hunt, Dave. *Beyond Seduction.* Eugene, OR: Harvest House Publishers, 1987.

Hunt, Dave. Q&A, "Would you please respond to CRI's *Journal* articles on biblical counseling by the Passantinos." *The Berean Call*, February 1996.

Hunt, Dave. Q&A, "The enclosed article by John H. Coe from R.C. Sproul's Ligonier Ministries' *Tabletalk* doesn't ring true to me. . . . Could you comment on this in your newsletter?" *The Berean Call*, February 1997.

Kirk, David L. Review of *The Social Importance of Self-Esteem. Santa Barbara News-Press* (9/30/89).

Johnson, Robert M. *A Logic Book*, Second Edition. Belmont, CA: Wadsworth Publishing Company, 1992.

Leifer, Ronald. *In the Name of Mental Health.* New York: Science House, 1969.

LeShan, Lawrence. *Association for Humanistic Psychology*, October 1984, p. 4.

Maslow, Abraham. *Toward a Psychology of Being*. Princeton: D. Van Nostrand Company, Inc., 1962, 1968.

Mecca, Andrew M., Neil J. Smelser and John Vasconcellos, eds. *The Social Importance of Self-Esteem*. Berkeley: University of California Press, 1989.

Mindess, Harvey. *Makers of Psychology: The Personal Factor*. New York: Insight Books, 1988.

Moffat, John D. "Is 'All Truth God's Truth'?" *The Christian Conscience* (May 1997).

O'Hara, Maureen. "A New Age Reflection in the Magic Mirror of Science." *The Skeptical Inquirer*, 13, 4 (Summer 1989), 368-374.

Passantino, Bob and Gretchen. "Psychology & the Church; Part One: Laying a Foundation for Discernment." *Christian Research Journal* (Winter 1995), 21-23, 35-38.

Passantino, Bob and Gretchen. "Psychology & the Church; Part Two: The 'Biblical Counseling' Alternative." *Christian Research Journal* (Spring 1995), 25-30.

Passantino, Bob and Gretchen. "Psychology & the Church; Part Three: Can Psychotherapy Be Integrated With Christianity?" *Christian Research Journal* (Summer 1995), 16-24, 39-40.

Passantino, Bob and Gretchen. "Psychology & the Church; Part Four: The High Cost of Biblical Compassion and Commitment." *Christian Research Journal* (Summer 1995), 18-22, 42-43.

Popper, Karl. "Scientific Theory and Falsifiability" in *Perspectives in Philosophy*. Robert N. Beck, ed. New York: Holt, Rinehart, Winston, 1975.

PsychoHeresy Awareness Letter, 1-5 (1993-1997). PsychoHeresy Awareness Ministries, Santa Barbara, CA 93110.

Riebel, Linda. "Theory as Self-Portrait and the Ideal of Objectivity." *Journal of Humanistic Psychology* (Spring 1982), 91-92.

Scriven, Michael quoted by Allen Bergin. "Psychotherapy Can Be Dangerous." *Psychology Today* (Nov. 1975), 96.

Sutherland, P. and P. Poelstra. "Aspects of Integration." Paper presented at the meeting of the Christian Association for Psychological Studies, Santa Barbara, CA, June 1976.

Szasz, Thomas. *The Myth of Psychotherapy*. Garden City: Doubleday/Anchor Press, 1978.

Torrey, E. Fuller. *The Death of Psychiatry*. Radnor: Chilton Book Company, 1974.

Van Til, Cornelius. *An Introduction to Theology*, Volume One. Philadelphia: Westminster Theological Seminary, 1947.

Vitz, Paul. "Christianity and Psychoanalysis, Part 1: Jesus as the Anti-Oedipus." *Journal of Psychology and Theology*, 12, 1 (1984), 4-14.

OTHER BOOKS FROM EASTGATE

Competent to Minister: The Biblical Care of Souls by Martin and Deidre Bobgan encourages believers to care for one another in the Body of Christ and demonstrates that God enables them to do so without incorporating the methods of the world. Contains much practical information for developing personal care ministries within the local fellowship of believers. Topics include overcoming obstacles to caring for souls, salvation and sanctification, caring for souls inside and out, ministering mercy and truth, caring for one another through conversation and practical helps, cautions to heed in caring for souls. This book exposes the professional, psychological intimidation that has discouraged Christians from ministering to one another during trials and temptations. It both encourages and reveals how God equips believers to minister to one another.

Four Temperaments, Astrology & Personality Testing by the Bobgans answers such questions as: Do the four temperaments give valid information? Are there biblically or scientifically established temperament or personality types? Are personality inventories and tests valid ways of finding out about people? How are the four temperaments, astrology, and personality testing connected? Personality types and tests are examined from a biblical, historical, and research basis.

Christian Psychology's War On God's Word: The Victimization Of The Believer by Jim Owen is about the sufficiency of Christ and how "Christian" psychology undermines believers' reliance on the Lord. Owen demonstrates how "Christian" psychology pathologizes sin and contradicts biblical doctrines of man. He further shows that "Christian" psychology treats people more as victims needing psychological intervention than sinners needing to repent. Owen beckons believers to turn to the all-sufficient Christ and to trust fully in His ever-present provisions, the power of His indwelling Holy Spirit, and the sure guidance of the inerrant Word of God.

OTHER BOOKS FROM EASTGATE

The End of "Christian Psychology" by Martin and Deidre Bobgan discusses research about the question, "Does psychotherapy work?" analyzes why Christians use psychological counseling, and gives evidence showing that professional psychotherapy with its underlying psychologies is questionable at best, detrimental at worst, and a spiritual counterfeit at least. The book includes descriptions and analyses of major psychological theorists and reveals that "Christian psychology" involves the same problems and confusions of contradictory theories and techniques as secular psychology. This book presents enough biblical and scientific evidence to shut down both secular and "Christian psychology."

PsychoHeresy: The Psychological Seduction of Christianity by Martin and Deidre Bobgan exposes the fallacies and failures of psychological counseling theories and therapies for one purpose: to call the Church back to curing souls by means of the Word of God and the work of the Holy Spirit rather than by man-made means and opinions. Besides revealing the anti-Christian biases, internal contradictions, and documented failures of secular psychotherapy, *PsychoHeresy* examines various amalgamations of secular psychologies with Christianity and explodes firmly entrenched myths that undergird those unholy unions.

12 Steps to Destruction: Codependency/Recovery Heresies by the Bobgans provides information for Christians about codependency/recovery teachings, Alcoholics Anonymous, Twelve-Step groups, and addiction treatment programs. All are examined from a biblical, historical, and research perspective. The book urges believers to trust the sufficiency of Christ and the Word of God instead of Twelve-Step and codependency/recovery theories and therapies.